THE

CONSTITUTION

OF THE

Reformed Church in America,

(KNOWN FOR A TIME AS THE "REFORMED DUTCH CHURCH," AND ALSO DESIGNATED IN THE ACT OF INCORPORATION, PASSED BY THE LEGISLATURE OF NEW YORK, APRIL 7TH, 1819, AS "THE REFORMED PROTESTANT DUTCH CHURCH.")

EMBRACING

THE CATECHISM, THE COMPENDIUM, THE CONFESSION OF FAITH, THE CANONS OF THE SYNOD OF DORDRECHT, AND THE LITURGY.

WITH AN APPENDIX,

CONTAINING

I. FORMULAS FOR THE USE OF CHURCHES,
II. RULES FOR THE RECEPTION OF MINISTERS,
III. RULES OF ORDER.

NEW YORK:
BOARD OF PUBLICATION,
Synod's Rooms, 103 Fulton Street.

PREFATORY NOTE.

In the year 1867 the Reformed Dutch Church, which is named in the following pages, dropped from its ecclesiastical name the word "Dutch," which was first formally assumed therein in the year 1792; and added the words "in America," so that the said Church might thenceforth be known as, "The Reformed Church in America." (See below, Chap. II., Art. 5, Sec. 1.) Yet, in order that the absolute identity of "The Reformed Church in America" with "The Reformed Dutch Church," might be subject to no possible doubt or dispute, it was also ordained, that the epithet "Dutch" should be retained in all those places in this Constitution in which it had previously been used; but should be inclosed in brackets, to indicate the purpose of the Church to discourage the ecclesiastical and popular use of that word as part of its name.

CONTENTS.

CHAPTER FIRST.

OF THE OFFICES IN THE CHURCH.

ARTICLE I.

Of Ministers of the Word.

ARTICLE II.

Of Teachers in Theology.

ARTICLE III.

Of the Offices of Elders and Deacons.

CHAPTER SECOND.

OF ECCLESIASTICAL ASSEMBLIES.

ARTICLE I.

Of Ecclesiastical Assemblies in General.

ARTICLE II.

Of Consistories.

ARTICLE III.

Of the Classis.

ARTICLE IV.

Of the Particular Synod.

CHAPTER THIRD.

OF CUSTOMS AND USAGES.

CHAPTER FOURTH.

OF DISCIPLINE.

CONTENTS.

INTRODUCTION.

For the maintenance of good order in the Church of Christ, it is necessary there should be certain *Offices* and *Assemblies*, and a strict attention to *Doctrines*, *Sacraments*, *Usages*, and *Christian Discipline*; of all which the following ecclesiastical ordinances particularly treat.

CHAPTER I.

OF THE OFFICES IN THE CHURCH.

The Offices in the Church of Christ are fourfold, viz:

1. The Office of Ministers of the Word.
2. The Office of Teachers of Theology.
3. The Office of Elders.
4. The Office of Deacons.

ARTICLE I.

Of Ministers of the Word.

SEC. 1. No person shall be allowed to exercise the office of a Minister without being thereinto regularly inducted, according to the Word of God, and the order established by the Church.

SEC. 2. Every person contemplating the work of the ministry, before he commences his course of Theological studies, shall furnish satisfactory evidence of his being a member in full communion and in good standing of a Reformed Protestant Church; of his piety, abilities, and literary attainments, and thereupon shall be admitted into one of the Theological Schools; and during the prosecution of his studies there, shall be subject to the rules and regulations thereof, and when he shall have completed the prescribed course and term of Theological studies shall be admitted to an examination according to the regulations of the schools, as established by General Synod; and if found qualified, shall receive a professorial certificate to that effect, which shall entitle him to an examination for licensure before the Classis to which he belongs.

SEC. 3. In the examination, strict attention shall be paid to the attainments of the Student, not only in the original languages of the Sacred Scriptures, in Biblical literature, in composition, and his method of sermonizing; but he shall be especially examined respecting his knowledge in Theology, his orthodoxy, his piety, and his views in desiring to become a preacher of the Gospel.

SEC. 4. Whoever, upon examination, shall be approved by the Classis, must, before he is licensed, attest his adherence to the do trines of the Gospel, by subscribing the following formula viz:

"WE, the underwritten, testify, that the Heidelbergh Catechism, and the Confession of the Netherland Churches; as also the Canons of the National Synod of Dordrecht, held in the years 1618 and 1619, are fully conformable to the Word of God. We promise moreover, that, as far as we are able, we will, with all faithfulness, teach and defend, both in public and private, the doctrines established in the standards aforesaid. And should ever any part of these doctrines appear to us dubious, we will not divulge the same to the people, nor disturb the peace of the Church, or of any community, until we first communicate our sentiments to the ecclesiastical judicatories under which we stand, and subject ourselves to the counsel and sentence of the same."

SEC. 5. After subscribing the aforesaid formula, the candidate shall be entitled to a certificate, or testimonial signed by the President of Classis, before whom the examination is held, containing a license to preach the Gospel.

SEC. 6. A candidate for the ministry is permitted only to preach the Word; but he may not, under any pretence whatever, administer the sacraments, nor can he be a delegate to represent a Church in any ecclesiastical assembly.

SEC. 7. Every candidate for the ministry is to consider himself under the immediate direction of the Classis which examined him, and subject to the control of the General Synod; and is to visit such congregations, and preach in those places to which the Classis or Synod shall send him; but, if no particular directions are given, he may preach at his own discretion in any congregation that shall invite him.

SEC. 8. Upon receiving a call from any particular congregation, a candidate shall be allowed time to consider the propriety of his accepting it. If more than one call is before him at the same time, he may determine which he will prefer; but if there be only one, it is expected he will not finally refuse the same, before having first referred his difficulties to the Classis, and obtained proper advice.

SEC. 9. A candidate who has accepted a call must offer himself to be examined for his becoming a Minister. In this final examination, besides a repetition of his previous trials in composition and sermonizing, the original languages of the Sacred Scriptures, Biblical literature, and his knowledge of Theology, as well Didactic as Polemic, he shall be interrogated respecting the nature and administration of the Sacraments, the duties of the ministry, and his knowledge of Ecclesiastical History, and of Church Government.

Sec. 10. Upon giving satisfaction in the examination, the candidate shall subscribe the following formula, viz:

"We, the underwritten, Ministers of the Word of God, residing within the bounds of the Classis of N. N., do hereby sincerely, and in good conscience before the Lord, declare by this our subscription, that we heartily believe, and are persuaded, that all the articles and points of doctrine contained in the Confession and Catechism of the Reformed [Dutch] Church, together with the explanation of some points of the aforesaid doctrine made in the National Synod held at Dordrecht in the year 1619, do fully agree with the Word of God. We promise, therefore, diligently to teach, and faithfully to defend the aforesaid doctrine, without either directly or indirectly contradicting the same by our public preaching or writings. We declare, moreover, that we not only reject all errors that militate against this doctrine, and particularly those which are condemned in the above mentioned Synod, but that we are disposed to refute and contradict them, and to exert ourselves in keeping the Church pure from such errors. And if hereafter any difficulties or different sentiments respecting the aforesaid doctrine should arise in our minds, we promise that we will neither publicly nor privately propose, teach or defend the same, either by preaching or writing, until we have first revealed such sentiment to the Consistory, Classis, or Synod, that the same may be there examined; being ready always cheerfully to submit to the judgment of the Consistory,

Classis, or Synod, under the penalty, in case of refusal, to be *ipso facto* suspended from our office. And, farther, if at any time the Consistory, the Classis, or Synod, upon sufficient grounds of suspicion, and to preserve the uniformity and purity of doctrine, may deem it proper to require of us a farther explanation of our sentiments respecting any particular article of the Confession of Faith, the Catechism, or the explanation of the National Synod, we do hereby promise to be always willing and ready to comply with such requisition, under the penalty above mentioned, reserving, however, to ourselves the right of an appeal, whenever we shall conceive ourselves aggrieved by the sentence of the Consistory, the Classis, or Particular Synod; and, until a decision is made upon such appeal, we will acquiesce in the determination and judgment already passed."

Sec. 11. Upon subscribing the aforesaid formula, a certificate, signed by the President, shall be given to the candidate; and the Classis before which the examination is held, shall fix a day for his ordination.

Sec. 12. The ordination shall be conducted by the Classis with proper solemnity; a sermon suited to the occasion shall be preached by him who has been appointed for that purpose; and the promises, directions, explanations of duty, with a laying on of hands, shall be agreeably to the form for that end expressly made and adopted.

Sec. 13. The *office of a Minister* is to persevere in prayer and the ministry of the Word; to dispense the Sacraments; to watch over his brethren the Elders and Deacons, as well as over the whole congregation; and lastly, in conjunction with the Elders, to exercise Christian discipline, and to be careful that all things be done decently and in good order. Every Minister must consider himself as wholly devoted to the Lord Jesus Christ in the services of the Church; and shall faithfully fulfil the obligations of his call, in preaching, catechizing, and visiting his flock; and be instant in season and out of season; and, by word and example, always promote the spiritual welfare of his people.

SEC. 14. No person shall be ordained to the ministry of the Word, without settling in some congregation, unless he be sent as a *Missionary* to Churches, or employed to gather congregations where none have as yet been established.

SEC. 15. A Minister of the Word, being once lawfully called, in manner before mentioned, is bound to the service of the sanctuary, as long as he liveth. Therefore, he shall not be at liberty to devote himself to a *secular vocation*, except for great and important reasons, concerning which the Classis shall inquire and determine.

SEC. 16. No Minister, relinquishing the service of his own Church, or being unattached to any particular congregation, shall be permited to *preach indiscriminately* from place to place, without the consent and authority of the Classis; in like manner, no Minister may preach or administer the Sacraments in any Church, other than his own without the consent of the Consistory of that Church.

SEC. 17. Ministers, who by reason of old age or habitual sickness and infirmities, either of mind or body, are not capable of fulfilling the duties of the ministry, may, upon application, and sufficient proof of such incapacity being made to the Classis, be declared *emeriti*, and be excused from all further service in the Church during such infirmity; reserving, however, to them the title, rank, and character which, before such declaration, they enjoyed. In all such cases, before the Classis declares any Minister *emeritus*, they shall require a stipulation in writing from the Consistory to which he belongs, under their common seal, and signed by their President, to pay such Minister annually, in half yearly payments, during his exemption from pastoral service, for his support. such sum as the Classis shall deem reasonable, having due regard to the stated salary of such Minister, and the situation and ability of the congregation.

Sec. 18. For the regular obtaining of dismissions, when a Minister has received and accepted a call from another place, it is required that a neighboring Minister of the same Classis to which the congregation belongs, be invited to be present, and superintend the dismission of the Minister from his congregation, countersign the instrument of dismission, and consider it as his duty to deliver the same, with a report upon the subject to the Classis; which report and document shall serve as a basis upon which the final dismission and certificate of the Classis shall be founded.

Sec. 19. All Ministers of the Gospel are equal in rank and authority; all are Bishops, or Overseers in the Church; and all are equal Stewards of the mysteries of God. No superiority shall therefore be ever claimed or acknowledged by one Minister over another, nor shall there be any lords over God's heritage in the Reformed [Dutch] Churches.

Sec. 20. Consistories of vacant congregations shall not invite or permit Ministers of other denominations in this country, whose characters and standing are not known, to preach within their bounds, unless they exhibit satisfactory evidence in writing, of a recent date, of their regular authority for that purpose, and their good standing; and in all doubtful cases, such Consistories shall consult a Standing Committee of Classis to be appointed for that purpose.

SEC. 21. The judicatories of the Church shall receive no Licentiates or Ministers under their care from any body of professing Christians who maintain doctrines different from those of the Reformed [Dutch] Church, without an open and explicit declaration, on their part, that they have renounced such doctrines as contrary to the Holy Scriptures, and the standards of our Church. If an application be made for admission of a Minister from a Church with which we are in correspondence, it shall be competent for the Classis, in case there be grounds of presumption against his doctrine and morals, to propose such inquiries as shall enable them to proceed with freedom in his case.

SEC. 22. With respect to foreigners who claim the privilege of preaching the Gospel, no Consistory shall be permitted to invite any one of them, of whatever denomination, to preach, before he shall lay his credentials before the Classis to which such Consistory is subordinate, and be regularly accepted and authorized by them to exercise his ministry within their bounds; and no Classis shall be permitted to receive and accredit such foreign Minister, unless he produce to them, besides ample and regular certificates of his license or ordination, and of his dismission and recommendations, of recent date, from the competent church judicatory, letters of recommendation also from some known respectable character, in the country from which he has emigrated, to his correspondent in this country, stating the authenticity of his credentials, and the good character and standing of the bearer, as a Minister of the Gospel, and that he is an advocate of the doctrines of grace professed by the Reformed Church.

ARTICLE II.

Of Teachers of Theology.

SEC. 1. As it is of the last importance that Professors of Theology should be sound in the faith, possess abilities to teach, and have the confidence of the Churches, they shall always, for the greater security, be chosen and appointed by a majority of votes in the General Synod only. To prevent, as far as possible, the unhappy consequences of partiality, haste, or undue influence in obtaining an office of such consequence to the Church, a nomination of one or more candidates shall be previously made, upon which the Synod shall fix a day when they will proceed to an election; provided that no appointment of a Professor in Theology shall ever be made on the same day on which he is nominated. An instrument certifying the appointment, and specifying the general duties of the office, shall be signed in the presence of the General Synod, by the President thereof, and by him be given, in the name of the Church, to the person elected.

SEC. 2. No person shall be appointed to the office of a Professor, who is not a Minister in good standing; and every Professor of Theology shall continue in his office during life, unless in case of such misbehavior as shall be deemed a violation of the obligations entered into at his appointment; or unless he voluntarily deserts or resigns his profession, or from age or infirmities becomes incapable of fulfilling the duties thereof; of all which the General Synod alone shall judge; and to that Synod a Professor of Theology shall always be amenable for his doctrine, mode of teaching, and moral conduct.

SEC. 3. No Professor of Theology shall be permitted to officiate until he shall have subscribed the following formula, viz:

"We, the underwritten, Professors of Sacred Theology in the Reformed [Dutch] Church, by this our subscription, uprightly, and in good conscience before God, declare, that we heartily believe, and are persuaded, that all the articles and points of doctrine contained in the Confession and Catechism of the Reformed [Dutch] Church, together with the explanation of some points of the said doctrine, made in the National Synod, held at Dordrecht, in the year 1619, do fully agree with the Word of God. We promise, therefore, that we will diligently teach, and faithfully defend the aforesaid doctrine; and that we will not inculcate or write, either publicly or privately, directly or indirectly, any thing against the same. As also, that we reject not only all the errors which militate against this doctrine, and particularly those which are condemned in the above mentioned Synod; but that we are disposed to refute the same, openly to oppose them, and to exert ourselves in keeping the Church pure from such errors. Should it nevertheless hereafter happen, that any objections against the doctrine might arise in our minds, or we entertain different sentiments, we promise that we will not, either publicly or privately, propose, teach, or defend the same, by preaching or writing, until we have first fully revealed such sentiments to the General Synod, to whom we are responsible; that our opinions may in the said General Synod receive a thorough examination, being ready always cheerfully to submit to the judgment of the General Synod, under the penalty, in case of refusal, to be censured by the said Synod. And whenever the General Synod, upon sufficient grounds of suspicion, and to preserve the uniformity and purity of doctrines, may deem it proper to demand from us a more particular explanation of our sentiments respecting any article of the aforesaid Confession, Catechism, or Explanation of the National Synod, we promise hereby to be always willing and ready to comply with such demand, under the penalty before mentioned; reserving to ourselves the right of rehearing, or a new trial, if we shall conceive ourselves aggrieved in the sentence of the General Synod; during the dependence of which new trial, we promise to acquiesce in the judgment already passed, as well as finally to submit, without disturbing the peace of the Churches, to the ultimate decision of the said General Synod."

SEC. 4. No Professor, while in office, shall have the Pastoral charge of any congregation, or be a member of any Ecclesiastical Assembly or Judicatory; but, as a Minister of the Gospel, may preach, and administer, or assist in administering the Sacraments in any congregation, with the consent of the Minister or Consistory.

SEC. 5. A Professor shall be at liberty to resign his office, by sending in his resignation to the President of General Synod, on the first day of any regular meeting, and giving six months' previous notice to the said President of his intention to do so.

ARTICLE III.

Of the Offices of Elders and Deacons.

SEC. 1. The *office of Elders* (besides what is common to them with the Ministers of the Word, expressed in Chapter I., Article 1., Section 13) is, to take heed that the Ministers, together with their fellow Elders and Deacons, faithfully discharge their respective duties; and also, especially before or after the Lord's Supper, as time and circumstances permit, and as shall be most for the edification of the congregation, to assist in performing visitations, in order particularly to instruct and comfort the members in full communion, as well as to exhort others to the regular profession of the Christian religion.

SEC. 2. The *office peculiar to the Deacons* is, diligently to collect the alms and other moneys appropriated for the use of the poor, and with the advice of the Consistory, cheerfully and faithfully to distribute the same to strangers, as well as to those of their own household, according to the measure of their respective necessities; to visit and comfort the distressed, and to be careful that the alms be not misused; of the distribution of which they shall render an account in Consistory, at such time as the said Consistory shall determine, and in the presence of so many of the congregation as may choose to attend. Should more be collected than the necessities of the poor may require, such surplus may, with the consent of the Consistory, be devoted to other purposes, connected with the wants of the Church.

SEC. 3. In all cases the Elders and Deacons shall be chosen from the male members of the Church, in full communion, and in forming new Churches, they shall be chosen by the male communicants; at whose election a neighboring Minister of the Reformed [Dutch] Church shall preside; and notice of the time and place of such election shall be published at least two Sabbaths, in the church or usual place of worship, previous to the election.

SEC. 4. The manner of choosing Elders and Deacons in Churches already organized, shall be as follows: A double number may be nominated by the Consistory, out of which the members of the Church in full communion may choose those who shall serve;—or, all the said members may unite in nominating and choosing the whole number without the interference of the Consistory;—or, the Consistory for the time being, as representing all the members, may choose the whole, and refer the persons thus chosen, by publishing them in the Church, for the approbation of the people. This last method has been found most convenient, especially in large Churches, and has long been generally adopted. But where that, or either of the other modes has for many years been followed in any Church, there shall be no variation or change, but by previous application to the Classis, and express leave first obtained for altering such custom.

SEC. 5. The Elders and Deacons shall be chosen to serve two years, except when chosen to fill a vacancy or vacancies occasioned by death, removal out of the congregation, resignation, or dismission from office, by the sentence of the Consistory; in either of which cases, the person or persons chosen to fill such vacancy or vacancies, shall serve for the residue of the term only.

SEC. 6. In order to avoid the inconvenience of an entire change at one time, the first Elders and Deacons of new congregations shall, at the first meeting of the Consistory after their ordination, be put into two classes, and the classes be marked Numbers 1 and 2, and the names to be put into each class shall be determined by ballot, and the term of service in Consistory of those in the first class shall expire at the end of the first year, so that one half of the whole number of Elders and Deacons may be elected annually. The same course shall be pursued by all the Consistories when they shall deem it requisite to enlarge the number of their Elders and Deacons, so far as relates to the additional number of members chosen by them. But this does not forbid the liberty of immediately choosing the same persons again, if from any circumstances it may be judged expedient to continue them in Consistory by a re-election.

CHAPTER II.

OF ECCLESIASTICAL ASSEMBLIES.

ARTICLE I.

Of Ecclesiastical Assemblies in general.

SEC. 1. The Ecclesiastical Assemblies which shall be maintained are,

1. Consistorial.
2. Classical.
3. Synodical.

SEC. 2. In these assemblies *ecclesiastical matters* only shall be transacted, and that in an ecclesiastical manner. A greater assembly shall take cognizance of those things alone which could not be determined in a less, or that appertain to the Churches or congregations in general, which compose such an assembly.

SEC. 3. The *transactions* of all Ecclesiastical Assemblies shall begin and conclude with prayer.

SEC. 4. Those who are delegated to attend the assemblies shall bring with them *credentials,* signed by those who send them; and such only shall be entitled to a vote.

SEC. 5. In all assemblies there shall be a President and Secretary. The business of the *Secretary* shall be to keep a faithful record of all the proceedings. The office of the *President* is to state and explain the business which is to be transacted; to preserve order; and in general to maintain that decorum and dignity becoming a judicatory of the Church of Christ.

SEC. 6. A Classis has the same *jurisdiction* over a Consistory, which a Particular Synod has over a Classis, and a General Synod over a Particular.

SEC. 7. Any individual conceiving himself to be personally aggrieved or injured by the decision of a lower Judicatory, may appeal therefrom to the judgment of an higher Judicatory; and any lower Judicatory, as a Consistory or Classis, esteeming itself aggrieved by the judgment or censure of a higher, enjoys the same privilege; but in such case the appeal must be made by the Judicatory as such when regularly convened, and not by any individuals belonging to it. Every individual appealing is bound to give his appeal, with the reasons thereof, in writing, to the Judicatory appealed from, or to the President thereof, at the most in ten days after notice of his intention; which notice is to be given at the time when he conceives himself aggrieved; and on default his appeal falls. The appeal of a Consistory or Classis may be made after the session of the Judicatory at which the decision appealed from was given; but it must be made known and the reasons of it stated in writing to the President, a reasonable length of time before the next meeting of the higher Judicatory to which the appeal is made. If the appellant give notice and satisfactory reasons to the President of the Judicatory to which the appeal is made, that he cannot attend at their next stated meeting, his appeal shall lie over to their next following stated meeting; but if no such notice and reason be given, and he does not appear to prosecute his appeal, it shall be considered as relinquished. It shall be the duty of the several lower ecclesiastical assemblies, from whose acts, proceedings, or decisions, any appeal is made, to transmit a certified copy of the act, proceeding, or decision so appealed from, signed by the President, and countersigned by the Clerk, together with the appeal and reasons accompanying the same, to the assembly appealed to, at the next regular meeting thereof.

SEC. 8. No member of an ecclesiastical assembly shall

be allowed to protest against any of its acts; any member who dissents from any such acts shall have a right to require the names of all the members present, who vote for or against the same, to be entered in the minutes, and published therewith for the information of all concerned.

SEC. 9. In order to prevent vexation and delay in the judicial proceedings of any ecclesiastical assembly by means of successive appeals in the progress of any trial or investigation, the party who may consider himself aggrieved by any decision, upon any incidental question which may arise before a final sentence is pronounced, may state his objections to such decision, and require to have the same noted in the minutes of the proceedings, to the end that he may avail himself thereof on an appeal from the final sentence, without arresting the progress of such investigation or trial. And in such cases every decision objected to, as well as the objections, shall be distinctly stated in the minutes of such assembly, and sent up with the appeal to the appellate Judicatory for review.

SEC. 10. Individuals who have voted in a lower court upon a case which is carried up by appeal, shall not be at liberty to vote upon the trial of the appeal in the higher courts.

SEC. 11. In any decision or adjudication of an ecclesiastical court which the minority, or any member of the minority, may regard as injuriously affecting the interests of truth, or of vital godliness, they may present the same to the Classis, Particular or General Synod, by way of complaint, for their examination and supervision.

SEC. 12. This complaint, if entertained, brings the whole proceedings in the case under the review of the superior Judicatory.

SEC. 13. No person shall be admitted to a seat in any of our ecclesiastical assemblies as an advisory member.

ARTICLE II.

Of Consistories.

SEC. 1. The Elders and Deacons, together with the Minister or Ministers, if any, shall form a Consistory, and the Minister shall preside at all consistorial meetings; but in the absence of a Minister, the Consistory may appoint one of the Elders to be their president *pro tem.*, and it shall be competent for the several Consistories to prescribe the mode and time of calling their meetings. If there be a plurality of Ministers, they shall preside in rotation.

SEC. 2. The Elders, with the Ministers of the Word, constitute what in the original Article of Church Government is properly called the Consistory. But as the Deacons have always in America, where the congregations were at first very small (See Synod Dord., art. 38), been joined with the Elders, and, wherever charters have been obtained, are particularly named as forming with them one Consistory, it is necessary to define their joint as well as respective powers. From the form of their ordination, it is evident that to the Elders, together with the Ministers of the Word, is committed the spiritual government of the Church; while to the Deacons belong the obtaining charitable assistance, and the distribution of the same, in the most effectual manner for the relief and comfort of the poor. When joined together in one board, the Elders and Deacons have all an equal voice in whatever relates to the temporalities of the Church, to the calling of a Minister, or the choice of their own successors; in all which they are considered as the general and joint representatives of the people. But in admitting members to full communion; in exercising discipline upon those who have erred from the faith, or offended in morals;

and in choosing delegates to attend the Classis, the Elders, with the Ministers, have alone a voice.

Sec. 3. No Consistory shall be constituted in any place without the previous advice and concurrence of Classis.

Sec. 4. Elders and Deacons shall be chosen annually, and the result of such election shall be published in the church, or usual place of worship of the congregation, three successive Sabbaths previous to their ordination, to the end that all lawful objections to such ordination may be offered to, and duly considered and adjudicated by the Consistory. A majority of the Consistory, regularly convened, shall be a quorum for the transaction of business; and, in like manner, a majority of Ministers and Elders, and also a majority of Deacons so convened, shall be a quorum respectively. It shall be competent for the Consistory, when an election shall have been omitted at the usual time, to appoint another time for that purpose, on an early day, giving the like notice as herein above prescribed. and in like manner for filling vacancies which may occur.

Sec. 5. The particular spiritual government of the congregation is committed to the Ministers and Elders. It is, therefore, their duty at all times to be vigilant, to preserve discipline, and to promote the peace and spiritual interest of the congregation. Particularly before the celebration of the Lord's Supper, a faithful and solemn inquiry is to be made, by the President, whether to the knowledge of those present, any member in full communion has departed from the faith, or in walk or conversation has behaved unworthy the Christian profession? that such as are guilty may be properly rebuked, admonished, or suspended from the privilege of approaching the Lord's Table, and all offences may be removed out of the Church of Christ.

SEC. 6. None can be received as members in full communion, unless they first shall have made a confession of their faith before the Minister, if any, and the Elders, or have produced a certificate of their being members in full communion of some Reformed Church; all such shall be published to the congregation, and be registered as regular members in the Church.

SEC. 7. In every congregation, a distinct and fair register shall be preserved by the Minister of every baptism and marriage there celebrated, and of all who are received as members in full communion. It shall be the duty of the several Consistories to make a statistical report to the Classis at their meeting immediately preceding the annual meetings of the Particular and General Synod, according to such formula as General Synod shall prescribe, and accompany the same with such remarks on the spiritual state of the congregation as they may deem proper.

SEC. 8. Every Consistory shall keep regular minutes of their meetings and proceedings, and shall lay such minutes, so far as the same relate to ecclesiastical proceedings, at least once a year, before the Classis with which they are connected, for their information.

SEC. 9. It shall be incumbent upon members of the Church, in removing from the bounds of one Church to another, to obtain a certificate of membership and dismission.

SEC. 10. Consistories possess the right of calling Ministers for their own congregations, except where otherwise provided for by charter. But in exercising this right, they are bound to use their utmost endeavors, either by consulting with the great Consistory or with the congregation at large, to know what person would be most acceptable to the people.

SEC. 11. A neighboring minister (if there be none

belonging to the Consistory) must be invited to superintend the proceedings, whenever a Consistory is desirous of making a call. The instrument is to be signed by the members of the Consistory, or by the President in the name of the Consistory; and if the Church be incorporated, it is proper to affix the seal of the corporation. When the call is completed, it must be laid by the Consistory before the Classis, and be approved by the same, before it can be presented to the person called; and if the call be accepted, for the purpose of receiving the approbation of the people, the name of such Minister shall be published in the church three Sabbaths successively, that opportunity may be given for stating lawful objections, if any there be.

SEC. 12. For the purpose of uniformity, the form of a call shall be as follows:

"To N. N.

"*Grace, mercy, and peace, from* GOD *our* FATHER, *and* JESUS CHRIST *our* LORD.

"WHEREAS the Church of Jesus Christ at ——, is at present destitute of the stated preaching of the Word, and the regular administration of the ordinances, and is desirous of obtaining the means of grace, which God hath appointed for the salvation of sinners, through Jesus Christ his Son: AND, WHEREAS, the said Church is well satisfied of the piety, gifts, and ministerial qualifications of you N. N., and hath good hope that your labors in the Gospel will be attended with a blessing: Therefore we [*the style and title of the said Church*] have resolved to call, and we hereby solemnly, and in the fear of the Lord, do call you, the said N. N., to be our pastor and teacher, to preach the Word in truth and faithfulness, to administer the holy Sacraments agreeably to the institution of Christ, to maintain Christian discipline, to edify the congregation, and especially the youth, by catechetical instructions; and, as a faithful servant of Jesus Christ, to fulfil the whole work of the Gospel ministry, agreeably to the Word of God, and the excellent rules and Constitution of our Reformed [Dutch] Church, established in the last National Synod, held at Dordrecht, and ratified and explained by the ecclesiastical judicatory under which we stand, and to which you, upon accepting the call, must with us remain subordinate.

"In fulfilling the ordinary duties of your ministry, it is expressly stipulated, that besides preaching upon such texts of Scripture as you may judge proper to select for our instruction, you also explain a portion of the Heidelbergh Catechism on the Lord's days, agreeably to the established order of the Reformed [Dutch] Church; and that you farther conform in rendering all that public service which is usual, and has been in constant practice in our congregation. The particular service which will be required of you is [*here insert a detail of such particulars, if any there be, which the situation of the congregation may render necessary; especially in case of combinations, when the service required in the respective congregations must be ascertained; or when the Dutch and English languages are both requisite, the proportion of each may be mentioned or left discretionary, as may be judged proper.*]

"To encourage you in the discharge of the duties of your important office, we promise you, in the name of this Church, all proper attention, love, and obedience in the Lord; and to free you from worldly cares and avocations, while you are dispensing spiritual blessings to us, we [*the Elders and Deacons, &c., the style and title of the Church*] do promise and oblige ourselves to pay to you the sum of ——, in —— payments, yearly and every year as long as you continue the Minister of this Church, together with [*such particulars as may refer to a parsonage or other emoluments*]. For the performance of all which, we hereby bind ourselves, and our successors, firmly by these presents. The Lord incline your heart to a cheerful acceptance of this call, and send you to us in the fulness of the blessing of the Gospel of peace!

"Done in Consistory, and subscribed with our names, this —— day of ——, in the year of ——."

Attested by N. N., Moderator of the call.

SEC. 13. Since it is deemed of the highest importance that there should be regular instruction on the great articles of the Christian faith, in order to preserve the truth, and to promote the prosperity of the Church, every Minister shall, in the ordinary morning or afternoon service on the Lord's day, explain the system of the Christian doctrine comprehended in the Heidelbergh Catechism adopted by the Reformed Churches, so that, if practicable, the explanation may be annually completed, but shall never be extended beyond the term of four years. The several Classes shall, at their stated meetings, preceding the annual meeting of General Synod, make strict inquiry whether the preceding part of this section has been fully complied with by every Minister, and if any Minister shall be found deficient, without sufficient reason, the Classis shall inflict such censure as they in their wisdom may judge the omission to merit; and the several Classes shall make a full and faithful report of the result of their inquiries and doings on this behalf to the Particular Synod.

SEC. 14. When any Minister shall be duly convicted of any offence which implicates the purity of his clerical character, and shall, in consequence of such conviction, be suspended from his office, and the conviction and suspension shall be sustained on a final appeal, his pastoral connection with the congregation in which he was settled shall, if the Consistory so elect, be *ipso facto* dissolved.

SEC. 15. Consistories which have hitherto combined with one or more neighboring Consistories, in making calls and having a Minister to serve in common, may not at pleasure break such combination; but whenever their situation and circumstances render them capable of severally calling a Minister, a representation thereof must be made to the Classis, and leave be first requested and obtained, before their former connections can be dissolved.

SEC. 16. When matters of peculiar importance occur, particularly in calling a Minister, building of Churches, or whatever relates immediately to the peace and welfare of the whole congregation, it is usual (and it is strongly recommended upon such occasions always) for the Consistory to call together all those who have ever served as Elders or Deacons, that by their advice and counsel they may assist the members of the Consistory. These, when assembled, constitute what is called the *Great Consistory*. From the object, or design of their assembling, the respective powers of each are easily ascertained. Those who are out of office have only an advisory or counseling voice; and, as they are not actually members of the board or corporation, cannot have a decisive vote. After obtaining the advice, it rests with the members of the Consistory to follow the counsel given them, or not, as they shall judge proper. But, unless very urgent reasons should appear to the contrary, it will be prudent and expedient, in all cases, to comply with the advice of those who, from their numbers and influence in the congregation, may be supposed to speak the language of the people, and to know what will be most for edification and peace.

ARTICLE III.

Of the Classis.

Sec. 1. A Classis consists of all the Ministers, and an Elder delegated from each Consistory within the bounds prescribed by Particular Synod. Collegiate Churches shall be entitled to an Elder for each ordinary worshiping assembly. To constitute a Classis, at least three Ministers and three Elders are required.

Sec. 2. Classis shall have the power of approving or disapproving calls; ordaining, suspending, and deposing Ministers, or dismissing them when called elsewhere. They shall have the power of forming new congregations, and determining the boundaries of congregations when such boundaries are contested; of continuing combinations of two or more congregations, the dissolution and change of the same; and a general supervising power in cases of appeal over the acts and proceedings of the Consistories within their bounds, which relate to the spiritual concerns of their particular Churches, and the conduct of any of the officers thereof.

Sec. 3. The peculiar prerogative of Classes, that of examining students of theology for their becoming candidates for the ministry, and of candidates for their becoming Ministers, is very important, and must always be attended to with great prudence, zeal, and fidelity. Every student of theology, when he shall have become prepared for examination for licensure, shall present himself for such examination to the Classis within whose bounds he resided when he entered upon his preparatory studies, and a candidate who has received a call, must be examined by the Classis under whose jurisdiction the Church that has made the call is placed.

SEC. 4. At every examination of a student or candidate by a Classis, it shall be the duty of two of the Deputati Synodi to be present, and no examination shall in any case proceed without the attendance of one Deputatus from another Classis, who shall see that the examination is performed with strictness, propriety, and justice, and duly report the same to the next Particular Synod. That the Deputati may obtain proper and timely notice, it shall be the duty of the President of the Classis, upon application being made to him for an examination (which application shall be made at least four weeks before the contemplated meeting of Classis), to send immediate information to the Deputati, and communicate the time and place when and where the same is to be held, in such manner that the Deputati shall be notified at least three weeks before such examination.

SEC. 5. Every Classis shall keep a book, in which the forms of subscriptions for candidates and Ministers of the Gospel are fairly written, which those who are examined and approved, shall respectively subscribe in the presence of the Classis. It shall also be the duty of every Classis, annually, to report to the Synod all persons who have been examined and licensed, as well as those who have been ordained; and also, all removals of Ministers from one place to another, or by death, which may have happened within the jurisdiction of such Classis, since the last session of Synod.

SEC. 6. Whenever the examination of a candidate for the ministry, the approbation of a call, or any other special business shall render an extraordinary meeting of the Classis necessary, it shall be the duty of the President of the Classis, upon application being made to him for that purpose, to call, by circular letters, the members together. And, whenever two Ministers and two Elders belonging to the Classis shall, upon *any occasion*, request in writing, under their hands, an extraordinary meeting, the President of the Classis may not refuse calling the same; provided that the expenses attending all extraordinary meetings of the Classis shall be always supported by the person or congregation at whose request, or for whose benefit, such session is held.

SEC. 7. The meetings of the Classis shall be semi-annual, at such times as they may respectively determine; and at every ordinary session, a sermon shall be preached.

SEC. 8. The Classis shall, at their meeting next preceding that of the Particular Synod, appoint delegates to attend the said Synod, and nominate delegates to the General Synod; and, at the same meeting, shall put to the Ministers and Elders, respectively, the following inquiries, and enter in detail the several answers given by each Minister and Elder, on the minutes, for the information of the higher judicatories:

1st. Are the doctrines of the Gospel preached in your congregation in their purity agreeably to the Word of God, the Confession of Faith, and the Catechisms of our Church?

2d. Is the Heidelbergh Catechism regularly explained agreeably to the Constitution of the Reformed [Dutch] Church?

3d. Are the catechising of the children and the instruction of the youth faithfully attended to?

4th. Is family visitation faithfully performed?

5th. Is the 5th Sec. 2d Art. 2d Chap. in the Constitution of our Church carefully obeyed?

6th. Is the temporal contract between Ministers and people fulfilled in your congregation?

SEC. 9. It shall be the duty of the several Classes to require from the respective Consistories a statistical table, filled up according to such formula as General Synod shall prescribe, accompanied with such remarks on the spiritual state of the congregation as they may deem proper.

SEC. 10. For the regular obtaining of dismissions of Ministers, it is required that a neighboring Minister of the same Classis to which the congregation belongs, be invited to be present and superintend the dismission of the Minister from his congregation, countersign the instrument of dismission, and consider it as his duty to deliver the same, with a report upon the subject, to the Classis; which report and document shall serve as a basis upon which the final dismission and certificate of the Classis shall be founded.

SEC. 11. When in the circumstances of foreign missionary fields, it shall be impracticable for a Classis to comply with all the requirements of the Constitution, the General Synod shall have full power to grant such dispensation as the wants of the case may demand.

ARTICLE IV.

Of the Particular Synod.

SEC. 1. Every Particular Synod shall comprehend a certain number of Classes, to be designated by the General Synod, and shall consist of a delegation of two Ministers and two Elders, from every Classis within its bounds; and seven Ministers and seven Elders, when regularly convened, shall constitute a quorum for the transaction of business; excepting those Synods which consist of not more than five Classes, in which case five Ministers and five Elders may form a quorum.

SEC. 2. To the Particular Synod belongs exclusively the power to form new Classes, to transfer a congregation from one Classis to another; to exercise a general supervising power in case of appeal over the acts and proceedings of the Classes within its bounds, and have cognizance of such matters as appertain to the spiritual welfare of all the Churches within its jurisdiction.

SEC. 3. Every Synod shall be at liberty to solicit and hold *correspondence* with its neighboring Synod or Synods, in such manner as shall be judged most conducive to general edification.

SEC. 4. Every Synod shall appoint a Deputatus primarius and secundus, from each Classis within its bounds, whose duty it shall be to superintend the examination of students in theology, and candidates for the ministry, to add a solemnity to the important work, and see that no undue liberty, superficial proceedings, or unnecessary rigor, be practiced. And it shall also be their duty, as Commissioners of Synod, to advise, exhort, and endeavor to persuade the Classis in all that respects the strict fulfillment of the important duty of examinations; but they are not invested with any authority to arrest the proceedings of any Classis who may act contrary to their advice; neither may they vote upon any question respecting any candidate that may be examined; but they are to keep regular minutes of the proceedings at their different examinations where they are present, and impartially report to the Synod whatever they may judge improper or wrong.

SEC. 5. A copy of the minutes of every session of the several Classes held since the last session of Synod, shall, at the opening of the Synod, be produced and laid on the table for the inspection of the members; the Particular Synod, from the several reports of the Classes, on the state of religion, shall prepare a Synodical report, to be presented to the General Synod, accompanied with the statistical tables of said Classes.

SEC. 6. The Particular Synod shall meet annually, at such time and place as they may determine, and special meetings may be held for the transaction of any extraordinary business, upon the written request of four Ministers to the President of the Synod; and in such case it shall be the duty of such President to give notice to the members of Synod of such meeting three weeks previous thereto, stating the particular object for which the Synod is to be convened.

ARTICLE V.

The General Synod.

SEC. 1. The General Synod shall consist of three Ministers and three Elders from each of the Classes, to be nominated by the Classes to the Particular Synod to which they belong, who shall have power to appoint the persons so nominated delegates to the General Synod; but, for good cause, may appoint other persons than those so nominated; or in case no nomination is made, may appoint the delegates for the Classis or Classes who shall have omitted to nominate. The Body thus constituted shall be called "The General Synod of the Reformed Church in America."

SEC. 2. The General Synod shall meet annually, at such time and place as they may determine; and twelve Ministers and twelve Elders, when regularly convened, shall be a quorum for the transaction of business.

SEC. 3. The General Synod shall have original cognizance of all matters relating to the Theological Schools, the appointment of Professors, and their course of instruction, the appointment of Superintendents of said schools, and the regulations thereof; and shall possess the power of regulating and maintaining a friendly correspondence with the highest Judicatories or Assemblies of other religious denominations, for the purpose of promoting union and concert in general measures which may be calculated to maintain sound doctrine, prevent conflicting regulations relative to persons under Church censure by the judicatories of either denomination, and to produce concert and harmony in their respective proceedings to promote the cause of religion and piety.

To the General Synod belongs the power to constitute Particular Synods, and to make any changes in the same, to exercise a general superintendence over the spiritual interests and concerns of the whole Church, and an appellate supervising power over the acts, proceedings, and decisions of the lower assemblies, relating to Christian discipline or the interests of religion, and the general welfare and government of the Church.

SEC. 4. If circumstances should require a meeting of the General Synod previous to the next ordinary meeting, the President shall, on a joint application of six or more Ministers requesting the same, call an extraordinary meeting at the place where the next ordinary meeting is appointed to be held, notice of which meeting shall be given to members of Synod at least three weeks previous to the time of such meeting, stating the particular business for which it is called, not however excluding the transaction of such other business as the Synod may deem proper.

CHAPTER III.

OF CUSTOMS AND USAGES.

ARTICLE I.

SEC. 1. The Sacrament of Baptism shall always be administered in the church, or some other place of public worship, at the time of public worship, and the form adopted for Baptism hitherto in use, shall in every case be retained. In cases, however, of the sickness of the parents, and especially of the infant, it is lawful to administer this Sacrament in private. But no private baptism shall be administered without the presence of at least one Elder, who shall accompany the Minister for that purpose, and the same form and solemnity shall be always used as in public baptism.

SEC. 2. Every Church shall observe such a mode in the administration of the Lord's Supper as shall be judged most conducive to edification; provided, however, after the sermon and usual public prayers are ended, the form for the administration of the Lord's Supper shall be read, and a prayer suited to the occasion shall be offered, before the members participate of the ordinance.

SEC. 3. The Sacrament of the Lord's Supper shall be administered at least twice a year, and it is recommended that the same be administered once every three months.

SEC. 4. For the purpose of uniformity in the order of worship, the following is to be observed by all the Churches:

1st. After a space for private devotion, the Minister shall introduce the public worship in the morning by invoking the Divine presence and blessing.

2d. Salutation.

3d. Reading the Ten Commandments, or some other portions of Scripture, or both.

4th. Singing.

5th. Prayer.

6th. Singing.

7th. Sermon.

8th. Prayer.

9th. Collection of Alms.

10th. Singing.

11th. Pronouncing the Apostolic Benediction.

The order of the afternoon and evening services shall be the same as the morning, excepting the reading of the Ten Commandments. The last service on the Lord's day shall conclude with the Christian Doxology.

SEC. 5. No Psalms or Hymns may be publicly sung in the Reformed [Dutch] Churches, but such as are approved and recommended by the General Synod.

CHAPTER IV.

OF DISCIPLINE.

ARTICLE I.

Of Discipline in General.

SEC. 1. Discipline is the exercise of the authority and the application of the system of laws, which the Lord Jesus Christ has appointed in His Church. Its objects are the removal of offences; the vindication of the honor of Christ; the promotion of purity and general edification of the Church; and also the benefit of the offender.

SEC. 2. All Christian discipline is spiritual, and nothing

shall be admitted as matter of accusation, or considered an offence, which cannot be proved to be such from Scripture, or the regulations of the Church founded on Scripture.

SEC. 3. All baptized persons are members of the Church, are under its care, and subject to its government and discipline.

ARTICLE II.

Of Private Offences.

SEC. 1. Private offences are those that are known to an individual only, or at most to a very few.

SEC. 2. Such offences are not to be immediately presented before a Church Judicatory, but the offender shall be dealt with according to the mode pointed out by our Lord in Matt. xviii. The same course shall be adopted in cases of personal or private injuries; but if, on due forbearance, these tender and Christian proceedings are unavailing, the whole matter shall be represented to the Judicatory to which the offender is amenable.

SEC. 3. Informers who have not taken these previous steps, shall be considered as guilty of an offence against the peace and order of the Church, and be censured accordingly.

ARTICLE III.

Public Offences.

SEC. 1. Public offences are those that require the cognizance of a Church Judicatory, as when they are so notorious and scandalous, that no private measures would obviate their injurious effects, or when, though originally known to one, or a few, the private measures taken have been ineffectual.

SEC. 2. When any person is charged with a crime, not by an individual, but by general rumor, the previous steps prescribed by our Lord in case of private offences are not necessary, but the proper judicatory is bound to take immediate cognizance of the matter.

SEC. 3. To constitute a general rumor, or *fama clamosa*, it is necessary—

1st. That it specify some particular sin or sins.

2d. That it should have obtained general circulation.

3d. That it be not transient.

4th. That it be accompanied with strong public presumption of its truth.

SEC. 4. In admitting accusations against a Minister or Elder, the rule prescribed in 1 Tim. 5: 19, shall always be observed, and accusers must come forward openly to support the charge.

SEC. 5. If Ministers of the Word have committed any public gross sin, which would render their appearance in the pulpit, under such circumstances, highly offensive, it shall be the duty of the Consistory, in order to prevent scandal, to shut the door against such criminal, and refer him to be tried by the Classis as soon as possible. The proceedings of the Consistory in such cases are at their peril, and are not to be considered as a trial, but only a prudent interference and binding over the person accused to the judgment of his peers. In case of like offences by the Elders and Deacons, they shall, upon trial and conviction, immediately be removed from their office by the Consistory.

SEC. 6. The following are to be considered as the *principal offences* that deserve the punishment of suspension, or removal from office, viz: False Doctrine or Heresy, Public Schisms, open Blasphemy, Simony, faithless Desertion of Office, or intruding upon that of another, Perjury,

Adultery, Fornication, Theft, Acts of Violence, Brawlings, Drunkenness, and scandalous Traffic; in short, all such sins and gross offences as render the perpetrators infamous before the world, and which in a private member of the Church would be considered as deserving excommunication.

SEC. 7. If any member of the Church shall be duly convicted of an infamous crime by any civil court, he shall, *ipso facto*, be debarred from the exercise of the peculiar functions of any ecclesiastical office with which he may be invested, and excluded from the privileges of the Church, until he shall have established his innocence, or manifested his repentance to the ecclesiastical judicatory to which he is amenable.

ARTICLE IV.

Of Process and Trial.

SEC. 1. Offences may be brought before a judicatory by individual accusation or common fame. In the former case, the process must be in the name of the accuser or accusers. In the latter no person need be named as the accuser.

SEC. 2. In exhibiting charges, the time, place, and circumstances shall be accurately stated in writing, that the accused may be enabled the better to defend himself.

SEC. 3. Great caution is to be exercised in receiving accusations where there is good reason to believe that they are preferred through passion or improper and unchristian motive; or where the accuser is under censure, or not of good character, or has the prospect of temporal advantage.

SEC. 4. All citations shall be issued and signed by the

President or Clerk, who shall also furnish citations for such witnesses as may be required on either side.

SEC. 5. A copy of the accusation shall be furnished to the accused at the time when the citation is served; which citation shall designate the time when, and place where, the accused shall put in his answer. Not less than ten days shall be allowed to intervene between the time appointed for receiving the answer of the accused and the trial of the case, unless by consent of all parties interested.

SEC. 6. When the accused refuses to obey the citation, he shall be cited a second time, which second citation shall always be accompanied by a notice, that if he still refuses to appear, at the time and place appointed, he shall not only be liable to censure for contumacy, but that the judicatory will proceed to the trial and decision of his case as if he were present.

SEC. 7. The trial shall be impartial. The witnesses, after being sworn or solemnly affirmed, shall be examined in the presence of the accused, and he shall be permitted to cross-examine them.

SEC. 8. To establish an accusation against any member of the Church, the testimony of more than one witness is required. The evidence shall be faithfully minuted, and with the sentence, or decision, be entered on the records, and the parties shall be allowed copies of the same at their own expense, if desired.

SEC. 9. No complaints in cases of scandal shall be admitted unless brought forward within the space of one year and four months after the crime shall be alleged to have been committed; excepting when it shall appear that unavoidable impediments prevented the bringing an accusation sooner.

SEC. 10. No professional counsel shall be permitted to

appear and plead in cases of process in any of the ecclesiastical courts. But if any accused person feel unable to represent and plead his own cause to advantage, he may request, or the President may appoint, any Minister or Elder belonging to the judicatory before which he appears, to prepare and conduct his cause as he may judge proper. But the Minister or Elder so engaged, shall not be allowed, after pleading the cause of the accused, to sit in judgment as a member of the judicatory.

SEC. 11. Such as obstinately reject the admonitions of the Consistory, or have been found guilty of the commission of a public or otherwise gross offence, shall be suspended from the Lord's Supper, which act of suspension may be published at the discretion of the Consistory; and being suspended and repeatedly admonished without discovering marks of repentance, the Church shall then proceed to the last remedy, namely, *Excommunication*, agreeably to the adopted form, and conformably to the Word of God. But no person shall be excommunicated without the previous advice of the Classis.

SEC. 12. *Before the Church proceeds to excommunication*, the obstinacy of the offender shall be publicly notified to the congregation, declaring his offences, together with the particular care and attention bestowed on him, by admonition, suspension from the Lord's table, and by repeated remonstrances. The congregation shall also be exhorted farther to admonish the delinquent, and to pray for him. This procedure shall be comprised in three several steps. In the *first* instance, the name of the offender shall not be mentioned, that he may in some measure be spared. In the *second*, with the advice of Classis, his name shall be expressed. In the *third*, the congregation shall be informed, that unless he repenteth, he will be excluded from the communion of the Church; so that if he remain obstinate, his excommunication may take place with their tacit approbation. The interval between these notifications shall be at the discretion of the Consistory.

SEC. 13. When an excommunicated person becomes *penitent*, and is desirous of being again reconciled to the Church, such desire shall be publicly declared to the congregation, either before the administration of the Lord's Supper, or at some other seasonable opportunity; that if no objections are offered, he may, on declaring his repentance, be publicly readmitted to a participation of the Lord's Supper, agreeably to the form appointed for that purpose.

SEC. 14. The General Synod shall have power to make all such rules and regulations as may be necessary for carrying the foregoing articles into execution, except where provision is thereby made for that purpose.

SEC. 15. No alteration shall ever be made to the foregoing articles, but by previous recommendation from the General Synod to the respective Classes, and the consent of a majority of the same to such proposed alteration, together with the final determination and resolution of the General Synod for the time being.

APPENDIX.

I.—FORMULARIES.

No. 1.

Form of a Professoral Appointment.

To the Rev. ——,

The General Synod of the Reformed Church in America, reposing confidence in your piety, learning and talents, have elected you a Professor in their Theological College at ———. The branches in which you are to instruct the youth committed to your charge are, ——— ———, with such modifications as the Synod may hereafter direct.

To free you from wordly cares and avocations, while discharging the duties of your office, we promise and oblige ourselves to pay to you the sum of ——— in ——— payments, yearly and every year, as long as you continue Professor in our Seminary as aforesaid. For the assumption of the powers, and the execution of the duties of your office in the Theological Department of the College, this is your commission, and may the Head of the Church render your labors useful and pleasant.

Signed by order of the Synod,

President.

Done in General Snoyd,
this ——day of——

No. 2.

Form of License.

To all whom it may concern, In the name of the Lord Jesus Christ, the great Head of the Church, we send greeting:

Be it known, that ———, having presented to the Classis of ——— testimonials of his literary and theological acquirements from the Professors of the Theological Seminary at ————, was admitted to an examination in the Hebrew and Greek languages, and the different branches of Theology as prescribed in the Constitution of the Reformed Church in America, and that the Classis being well satisfied of his gifts, piety, and qualifications to preach the Gospel, did, in the name of the Lord Jesus Christ, the King and Head of the Church, resolve that the said ——— be, and hereby is, allowed and authorized as a candidate for the sacred ministry within their bounds, and wherever the Providence of God may call him to preach the Gospel of our blessed Lord and Saviour. And the said Classis recommend him to the esteem and attention of all those to whom these presents may come, as well qualified to preach a crucified Saviour.

The Classis do fervently pray, that the great Head of the Church may further qualify him for the work of the ministry, and make him eminently useful in that part of his vineyard where he may be called.

Done in Classis, in the ——— on this ——— day of ——— 18—.

President.

Clerk.

No. 3.

Form of Testimonial of Ordination.

In the name of the Lord Jesus Christ, the great Head of the Church, to all whom it may concern, we send greeting:

Be it known that ——— was admitted by the Classis of ——— to an examination on the different branches of Theology, as prescribed in the Constitution of the Reformed Church in America, preparatory to ordination, and the Classis being well satisfied with his gifts, piety and qualifications to preach the Gospel and administer the Sacraments, did in the name of the Lord Jesus Christ, the King and Head of the Church, resolve that the said ——— be ordained to the Gospel ministry, and in conformity to said resolution did, on the ——— day of ——— set him apart solemnly to the work of the sacred ministry, according to the rites and forms of the Reformed Church, and receive him into ministerial communion. And the said Classis do recommend him to the esteem and attention of all those to whom these presents shall come, as qualified to preach the Gospel, and to administer the Sacraments of our Lord Jesus Christ.

The Classis do fervently pray that the great Head of the Church may abundantly qualify him for the work of the ministry, and make him eminently useful in that part of the vineyard where he may be called to labor.

Done in Classis, at ——— on this ——— day of ——— 18——.

President.

Clerk.

No. 4.

Form of a Certificate of the Dismission of a Minister from his Congregation.

This certifies that the undersigned, by request, was present at a meeting of the Consistory of the Church of ———, on the ——— day of ———, A.D., ———, and superintended the proceedings thereof, when it was resolved that an application be made to the Classis of ——— for a dissolution of the pastoral connection between the Rev. ——— and said Church; and that the Rev. ——— declared his concurrence in such application.

No. 5.

Form of Certificate of Dismission of Church Members.

This certifies, that ——— is a member in full communion of the Reformed Church of ———, in good and regular standing; as such ——— is at ——— own request, dismissed, for the purpose of connecting ——— with the ——— Church of ———, to whose Christian fellowship and confidence ——— is hereby affectionately commended; and when received by them, ——— peculiar relation to this Church shall cease.

By order of Consistory.

———, *President.*

Given at ———, ———, 18—.

☞ **This Certificate is valid only for one year from its date, except where there has been no opportunity of presenting it.**

No. 6.

Form of the Register of Baptisms.

DATE OF BAPTISM	NAMES OF THE BAPTIZED	NAMES OF THE PARENTS	TIME OF BIRTH	REMARKS

N.B.—In recording the name of the Mother, give her family or maiden name.

No. 7.

Form of Certificate of Marriage.

To all whom it may concern; This certifies that the Bonds of Marrriage between ——— and ———were by me confirmed, according to the usuages of the Reformed Church in America, on the ——— day of ———, in the year of our Lord one thousand eight hundred and ——.

Given at ———, this ——— day of ———, A.D., 18—.

{ *Minister of the Reformed Church in* ——.

No. 8.

Form of Consistorial Report.

ANNUAL REPORT of the Church of ——

Census	Number of Families	
Communicants — Rec'd	On Confession	
	On Certificate	
Communicants	Dismissed	
	Suspended	
	Died	
	Total now in Communion	
Bap.	Infants	
	Adults	
C. & B. C.	Number of Catechumens	
	Number in Biblical Instruction	
Sab. Sch.	Average Number of Scholars	
Contributions	Religious and Benevolent Purposes	
	Congregational Purposes	

Dated ——, 18—

——, *Pastor.*

No. 9.

Form of a Classical Report.

CHURCHES	PASTORS	Census	Communicants						Bap.		C. & B. C.		S. S.	Contributions		OFFICE ADDRESS
			Rec'd													
		Number of Families	On Confession	On Certificate	Dismissed	Suspended	Died	Total now in Communion	Infants	Adults	Number of Catechumens	Number in Biblical Instruction	Average Number of Scholars	Religious and Benevolent Purposes	Congregational Purposes	

Remarks on the spiritual state of the congregation.

The name of the Stated Clerk of the Classis to be underscored, or the letters S. C. appended to his name.

No. 10.

Form of the Citation of a Person accused.

By order of the ——,* you, Mr. A. B. ——,† are hereby summoned ‡ to appear before said ——, and answer to the charge herewith presented, at ——, on the —— day of ——, at —— o'clock ——.

Signed, ——, *Pres.*
——, *Clerk.*

Done in ——, *at* ——, *this* —— *day of* ——, 18—.

No. 11.

Form of the Citation of Witnesses.

By order of the —— § you, Mr. A. B. ——,‖ are hereby summoned ** to appear before the said ——, at ——, on the —— day of ——, and at —— o'clock in the ——, to give your testimony in the case of C. D., presently under process for censure by said ——.

Signed, ——, *Pres.*
——, *Clerk.*

---

* Consistory of the Reformed Church at ——, or the Classis of ——.

† Member of, or Elder, or Deacon in said Congregation; or Minister at ——, under the inspection of said Classis.

‡ If the process be raised at the instance of a party complaining add, after "summoned," at the instance of C. D.

§ Consistory of the Reformed Church at ——, or the Classis of ——.

‖ Member of, or Elder, or Deacon in said Congregation; or Minister at ——, under the inspection of said Classis, and if the witness belongs to a different judicatory, the blank is to be filled up accordingly.

** If the process be raised at the instance of a party complaining, add, after the word "summoned," at the instance of C. D.

II.—THE RECEPTION OF MINISTERS.

1. No licentiate nor ordained minister, from any other ecclesiastical body, shall be received into any Classis until, either by documentary evidence or examination, they shall have become satisfied of his competent literary qualifications; nor until upon examination, in the presence of a deputatus, they shall also become fully satisfied of his competent theological attainments, his piety, soundness in the faith and ability to teach, and shall have received his entire assent to the standards of our Church, as to doctrine and discipline.

2. That if any candidate or minister, applying for admission into any Classis, shall, in the judgment of Classis. have sought and obtained licensure or ordination from any ecclesiastical organization for the sake of an easier admission into our Church than upon the strict terms enjoined upon our own students at New Brunswick, it shall be considered a disqualification, to be removed only by a dispensation from the General Synod.

4. No licentiate shall be received as a candidate under the care of Classis, or be privileged to minister in, or receive a call from our Churches, unless he shall have spent the same amount of time in actual attendance on theological instruction that is required from our own students; and any deficiency in this respect shall be made up by study in our own Seminary.

4. It is enjoined on the Standing Committee on Doctrine in the several Classes, when a vacancy occurs, to send to such vacant church, immediately, a list of the licentiates of our own Seminary, and to use their endeav-

ors to procure for them an early hearing; and it is recommended to the consistories of our Churches, in all cases, promptly to endeavor to obtain their services.

5. Whenever a Church becomes vacant, it shall be the duty of the Classis to exercise guardianship over it, and, when requested by the consistory, to supply it as far as practicable by their personal services—thus preventing the disorganizing influence of casual and indiscriminate ministrations; and to maintain such a supervision over it, and minister such aid as is necessary to carry out these rules, and such as a destitute Church is entitled to claim from its very relations.

6. No foreign minister shall be received on mere private letters of introduction or recommendation; but, in all cases, full ecclesiastical certificates shall be required.

7. No foreign minister shall be received by any Classis, unless he shall have undergone a probation of one year under the care of a Classis, and shall then present the same testimonials, and undergo the examination required by the first of these rules.

8. These rules shall be inserted in some conspicuous place in the minute books of the respective Classes.

III.—RULES OF ORDER.

1. At every stated meeting of the Synod, a sermon shall be preached by the last President, either before his opening the session with prayer, or at some time afterward, which the Synod shall deem most convenient. If the last President and the Adsessor be absent, the oldest minister present shall take his place and perform the above duties.

2. The President and Adsessor shall be elected by ballot, by a majority of all the members present; and if after the first vote there is no election, the choice shall be made from the two who have the highest number of votes. The clerks shall be elected by plurality.

3. The duties of the President shall be:

1. To take the chair at the hour to which the Synod stands adjourned.

2. To open and conclude with prayer.

3. To direct the Clerk immediately after a quorum has appeared to call the roll.

4. To censure absentees when their absence shall be judged not to have been necessary.

5. To propound the subjects for deliberation.

6. To confine speakers to the point, and to save them from unnecessary interruption.

7. To state and put the question, when the members are prepared to vote.

8. To prevent members from leaving the Synod without permission.

9. To decide questions of order, subject, however, to an appeal to the house by any two members.

10. To give the casting vote in all equal divisions.

11. And, in general, to maintain the order and dignity becoming the judicatory of the Church of Christ.

4. After calling the roll, the minutes of the last sitting shall be read, and considered as open to correction. The business on the minutes of the last meeting or sit-

ting, shall, without powerful reasons, be taken up and concluded first, in the order in which it stands, before any new business be introduced.

5. A motion made must be seconded, and afterwards repeated, or read aloud from the Chair, before it is debated; and every motion, except a motion for adjournment, shall be reduced to writing if any member require it.

6. An amendment may be made to any motion, and it shall be decided before the original motion. It may be, in its turn, suspended by an amendment to itself, which must first be considered and decided. But no additional amendment to an original motion can be received until the previous one has been disposed of.

7. When a question is under debate, no motion shall be received except to adjourn, to lay on the table, to postpone indefinitely, to postpone to a certain time, to commit to a standing committee, to a select one, or to the committee of the whole, to amend, or for the previous question; which motions shall have precedence in the order stated.

8. When the previous question is moved and seconded, it shall be in this form: "Shall the main question be now put?" and until it be decided all amendments and debate shall be inadmissible. If the vote be in the *affirmative*, the original motion shall be immediately put without further amendment or debate. But if there be an amendment or amendments pending at the time, the question shall first be taken on such amendment or amendments in their proper order, without debate. If the vote be in the *negative* the debate shall continue as before.

9. A question shall not be called up or reconsidered at

the same session of the Synod at which it was decided, unless by consent of two-thirds of the members present.

10. No member shall be allowed to protest against any of the acts of the Synod; but any member who dissents from any such acts shall have a right to require the names of all the members present, who vote for or against the same, to be entered in the minutes, and published therewith for the information of all concerned. In other cases, the yeas and nays shall not be recorded unless on the demand of one-fifth of the members present.

11. The mover and seconder of a motion may withdraw it before debate has commenced on it, but not afterwards, unless by leave of Synod.

12. In filling blanks, when various motions are made, the vote shall always be first on the highest number and longest time.

13. Every member shall rise and address himself to the President only, closely attending to the subject in debate, avoiding all personal reflections; and no member, without the special permission of the Synod, shall speak more than twice on the same subject. When two or more members rise to speak at the same time, the President shall determine who of them shall be heard first.

14. After the President has begun to take the vote, or the Clerk to call the roll on a division of the house, no debate nor remark shall be allowed.

15. A motion to adjourn or to lay on the table, and all motions in relation to priority of business, shall be decided without debate. The motion to postpone or to commit shall preclude all debate of the main question.

16. When an appeal is taken from a decision of the Chair on a point of order, the President shall have the

right to explain the grounds of his decision, but the appeal shall be decided by the house without debate.

17. No member shall leave the Synod to return home or for other business without their consent; nor shall members, without express permission, engage in private conversation, go from or change their seats during the transaction of business; interrupt another when he is speaking, except he be out of order, or to correct mistakes and misrepresentations; and if any member act indecently or disorderly, contrary to these rules, the President shall reprove or otherwise censure him, as the Synod shall judge proper; the member still having the privilege, if he think himself denied any right or unjustly blamed by the President, of respectfully and modestly requiring the decision of the house in the case.

18. All the sittings of General Synod shall be concluded by regular adjournment and prayer.

19. At the close of every session of General Synod the roll shall be called, and the names of those who are absent without permission shall be recorded.

20. *Standing Committees:*

(1.) Professorate.
(2.) Overtures.
(3.) Synodical Minutes.
(4.) Domestic Missions.
(5.) Foreign Missions.
(6.) State of Religion.
(7.) Education.
(8.) Judicial Business.
(9.) Widows' and Disabled Ministers' Funds.
(10.) Publication.
(11.) Nominations.

(12.) Correspondence.

(13.) Acconnts.

(14.) Leave of Absence.

(15.) Board of Direction.

21. All distinctive titles or appendages to the names of members of Synod shall be omitted in recording the minutes of this Synod; such distinctive title being prefixed or appended to the name of the member in the list of members constituting the Synod.

22. *Primarii and Secundi:*

(1.) When a Primarius shall find it impracticable to attend the judicatory to which he is delegated, it shall be his duty as soon as may be, to notify a Secundus, and when he shall take his seat it shall not be vacated to give place to the Primarius.

(2.) At the commencement of the session, the members delegated, whether Primarii or Secundi, shall be recognized and recorded, but when the Primarius shall appear at any subsequent period of the session, then the Primarius shall take the seat of the Secundus, and the Secundus shall not be considered a member again, unless by request of the Primarius, and express permission obtained by the Synod.

23. *Judicial Business:*

(1.) Any appeal, complaint, or other judicial business, which shall be presented or reported to the Synod, shall be first referred, with all the papers and documents appertaining thereto, to the Committee on Judicial Business, who shall inquire whether the same has been regularly brought before the Synod, and whether all the constitutional steps in the case have been taken, and, if the same shall be found in order, they shall digest and arrange all the papers and documents connected therewith, that the subsequent proceedings in the case before the Synod may be regular and sytematic; provided, nevertheless, that the said committee shall be required to report upon every matter that may be referred to them.

(2.) Whenever any case thus reported shall be taken up for trial, the President shall solemnly announce from the Chair that the Synod is about to proceed to the consideration of judicial business, and enjoin on the members to recollect and regard their character as judges of the highest court of Jesus Christ on earth, known to the Constitution of the Reformed [Dutch] Church; after which it shall not be in order, during the pending of such trial, to transact any legislative business bearing on the case.

(3.) In recording their decision, it shall be the duty of the court who have tried any judicial business in the original case, or by appeal, to set forth at length the reasons thereof, that the record may exhibit, as far as practicable, every thing that had an influence on their judgment; a certified copy of which, with the act of proceeding appealed from, shall be sent up by them to the court to whom the appeal may be taken. Such inferior court shall also be permitted to send a commissioner to the Synod, for the purpose of making any explanations relative to said case, it being expressly understood that in every case the original parties be not lost sight of in any stage of trial.

(4.) In taking up an appeal, after having ascertained that the appellant has conducted it regularly, the following shall be the order of trial:

[1.] The sentence appealed from shall be read.

[2.] The appeal and reasons of appeal shall be read.

[3.] All the documents in the case shall be read, in the order prescribed by the Committee on Judicial Business.

[4.] The original parties shall be heard, commencing with the appellant.

[5.] The commissioner of the inferior judicatory which has tried the appeal may be heard in explanation of the grounds of their decision, and of the manner of their proceeding in the case.

[6.] The appellant may be heard in reply.

(5.) After all the parties shall have been fully heard, and all the information gained by the Synod which shall be deemed necessary, the parties shall withdraw, when the roll shall be called, that every member may have an opportunity to express his opinion on the case, after which the final vote may be taken.

(6.) The decision may be either to confirm or reverse, in whole or in part, the judgment of the inferior judicatory, or to remit the cause with instructions or for a new trial.

(7.) In the trial of all judicial business brought before the Synod, by complaint or reference, the same order of proceeding shall be observed, as far as practicable, as in cases of appeal, but no complaint shall be entertained unless notice of the same shall have been given before the rising of the judicatory whose act is complained of, or within ten days thereafter.

24. *Religious Exercises :*

(1.) The afternoon of the first day shall be devoted to exercises of prayer and praise.

(2.) The first half hour of each subsequent morning session shall be so spent after the reading of the minutes.

(3.) The Lord's Supper shall be observed on the afternoon of the second day.

(4.) A sermon in behalf of the benevolent operations

of the Church shall be preached on the evening of the sixth day of the session.

25. The morning of the third day of the session shall be devoted to the purpose of hearing from the secretaries of our various Boards such oral statements as they shall see fit to make; after which, an opportunity shall be afforded for a free interchange of opinion and feeling among the members of the Synod in regard to the benevolent operations of the Church.

26. A rule of order may be suspended for the time by unanimous consent.

27. These rules (except 22, 23, 24, and 25) shall be read at the opening of each General Synod.

INDEX TO THE CONSTITUTION.

DIGEST

OF THE

Laws of the General Synod

OF THE

REFORMED CHURCH IN AMERICA,

TO THE

SESSION IN JUNE 1869, INCLUSIVE.

Prepared by a Committee appointed for the purpose.

PUBLISHED BY ORDER OF SYNOD.

NEW YORK:
BOARD OF PUBLICATION
REFORMED CHURCH IN AMERICA,
SYNOD'S ROOMS, 150 WILLIAM STREET.
1869.

CONTENTS.

For pages and fuller statements of sections see the index at the close of the volume.

DIGEST.

CHAPTER I.

NAME OF THE CHURCH.

The Reformed Church in America

The incorporation of the General Synod granted by the Legislature of the State of New York, April 7th 1819, was under the designation of "The Reformed Protestant Dutch Church."

At the session of Synod in June, 1866, a Committee was appointed to consider the propriety of a change in the name of the Church. The Committee reported in June, 1867. Their Report is printed as an Appendix to the Minutes of Synod of that year. The action of Synod accepting the change proposed, and referring it to the Classes, is contained in the same Minutes (June, 1867), pp., 239–242. The Classes reported, twenty-five affirmatively and six negatively, to Synod in an extra session Nov. 1867. See Minutes of the session, Vol. XI., pp. 331-335. A Committee was appointed to secure the necessary legislative enactments. A memorial to the Legislature of the State of New York was adopted in June, 1868, Minutes, Vol. XI., pp. 464–466. At the session of Synod in June, 1869, information was received of the passing of the following act by the Legislature :

"*The People of the State of New York, represented in Senate and Assembly, do enact as follows:*

. The ecclesiastical body hitherto incorporated and known by the corporate title of the General Synod of the Reformed Protestant Dutch Church, shall hereafter be designated and known by the corporate title of the General Synod of the Reformed Church in America, and as such exercise and enjoy all the rights and powers it has hitherto possessed.

This act shall take effect immediately."

Vol. XI., p. 625.

CHAPTER II.

CONSTITUTION OF THE CHURCH.

The Constitution of the Reformed Church includes, 1. The Revised Rules of Church Government. 2. Her Doctrinal Standards, consisting of the Confession of Faith, the Heidelberg Catechism and Compendium, and the Canons af the Synod of Dort. 3. The Liturgy, Vol. IV., pp. 425, 426.

CHAPTER III.

CONSISTORIES.

SEC. I. *To obey Sec. 20, Art. 1, Chap. 1, of Constitution.*

The General Synod enjoins upon the Consistories of the several churches strictly to adhere to the article of the Constitution in relation to the Standing Committee of Classis in relation to vacant congregations. Vol. V., p. 58.

SEC. II. *Synodical Minutes are to be examined.*

It is recommended to all the Consistories under the

supervision of this Synod, to appoint a committee annually, as near the 1st of June as possible, to be called the Committee of Synodical Minutes, whose duty it shall be, as soon after the authenticated copies of the Minutes have been received as possible, to examine the Minutes of Particular and General Synods, and report to their several Consistories the subjects that require their action. Vol. V., p. 162.

SEC. III. *To seek aid from the Board of Missions, through Classis.*

It is recommended to every church now receiving aid from the Board of Missions, or hereafter to receive aid from the same, first to make application to the Classis within whose bounds it is situated, and that such Classis be requested to consider the case, and if, in their opinion, possessing a fair claim to the measure of aid which said church specifies, recommend it to the Board to allow them the said appropriation. Vol. V., p. 290.

SEC. IV. *To endeavor to support Beneficiaries recommended by themselves.*

When any church recommends a beneficiary to the funds of the Education Board, or any other funds at the disposal of this Synod for classical or theological education, said church or consistory shall first make an effort to sustain such young man, and report to the Classis with which such church is connected, to what extent they shall be able to assist. Vol. VI., p. 231.

SEC. V. *To revoke a recommendation when thought expedient.*

Special care shall be exercised by Consistories and Classes in recommending young men to the Education

Fund: and that if at any time a Consistory or Classis shall become convinced of the unfitness of any person recommended by them, said Consistory or Classis are expected to revoke their recommendation as soon as possible. Vol. V., p. 232; Vol. VI., p. 232.

SEC. VI. *Have power to decide on the validity of Romish baptism.*

Whereas, the right of receiving members into the church belongs constitutionally to the consistories therefore

Resolved, That the question of the validity of Roman Catholic baptism be left to the different consistories. Vol. IV., p. 403.

SEC. VII. *Enjoined to present to Classes annual written and particular reports on the state of religion within their bounds.*

Resolved, That it be enjoined through the medium of the Particular Synods and the several Classes, upon the several Consistories, to present annually to their respective Classes a statistical account of their congregations, and also an account of vital religion throughout their societies. Vol. I., 1809, p. 23; 1814, p. 74; Vol. III., p. 45.

SEC. VIII. *Duty in regard to Sabbath schools.*

It is recommended to the several ministers and consistories in our Church, where it is not already the case, to take the school or schools formed of teachers and scholars belonging to their churches and congregations under their oversight and care. Vol. III., p. 278.

SEC. IX. *To defray the expenses of their ministers and elders attending the judicatories of the Church.*

Resolved, That it be recommended to the consistories

that they defray the expenses of their ministers and elders, who attend from time to time the several judicatories of the Church. Vol. I., 1797, p. 14; 1814, p. 34; 1815, p. 74.

SEC. X. *To endeavor to obtain an interest in the Widows' fund for their ministers.*

Synod, desirous that *all* their ministers may, if praccable, become interested in the Widows' Fund, do *Resolve*, that in cases in which ministers may find it inconvenient themselves to become subscribers to this Fund, it be recommended to the consistories to secure for their pastors an interest therein, by subscribing on their behalf. Vol. V., pp. 191, 297; Vol. VI., p. 142.

SEC. XI. *To sustatn the benevolent operations of the Church.*

Resolved, That in the judgment of this Synod all pastors and consistories are under solemn obligation to the Church, and those looking to her for aid, to carry out faithfully, and in the most efficient way practicable, the arrangement for meeting the calls of our benevolent operations.

Resolved, That this Synod highly approve and commend to the churches, as one of the most efficient means of collecting the charities of the Church, the plan of dividing each congregation into sections, and appointing persons (both males and females) to call upon every member in each section, periodically, for contributions to benevolent objects. Vol. VI., pp. 29, 30.

SEC. XII. *To render full reports of membership and contributions.*

Resolved, That it be enjoined on the consistories to

render full reports of membership and contributions. Vol. IX., p. 57.

SEC. XIII. *To procure all publications of the Board of Publication for Pastors' libraries.*

Resolved, That this Synod recommend to each consistory of our Church to procure all the publications of our Board of Publication * * * to be placed in the pastor's library of each church, and to remain there as the property of the church. Vol. IX., p. 240.

SEC. XIV. *When there is no settled Pastor, the consistory is to have collections ordered by Synod taken up in the church.*

Resolved, That it is the duty of * * * every consistory where there is no settled pastor, to see to it that the collections ordered by Synod are regularly taken up in the churches under their care. Vol. XI., p. 504.

CHAPTER IV.

OLASSES.

SEC. I. *To hold a free conversation on the State of Religion.*

Each Classis is requested to hold, at its stated meetings, immediately preceding the annual meeting of the General Synod, a free conversation on the state of religion in their congregations; and that on some day of such meeting, each Classis, as such, spend one hour in special prayer, in behalf of the interests of vital religion within our bounds. June, 1820, p. 58.

SEC. II. *Their Committees on Consistorial Minutes may report on any matters demanding Classical action.*

According to the Constitution, it is the duty of the Committee on Minutes of Consistories to report for correction, adjudication, or advice, all matters which may demand the action of Classis. Vol. V., p. 506.

SEC. III. *On the reception of Ministers.*

1. No licentiate nor ordained minister, from any other ecclesiastical body, shall be received into any Classis until, either by documentary evidence or examination, they shall have become satisfied of his competent literary qualifications; nor until upon examination, in the presence of a deputatus, they shall also become fully satisfied of his competent theological attainments, his piety, soundness in the faith and ability to teach, and shall have received his entire assent to the standards of our Church, as to doctrine and discipline.

2. That if any candidate or minister, applying for admission into any Classis, shall, in the judgment of Classis, have sought and obtained licensure or ordination from any ecclesiastical organization for the sake of an easier admission into our Church than upon the strict terms enjoined upon our own students at New Brunswick, it shall be considered a disqualification, to be removed only by a dispensation from the General Synod.

3. No licentiate shall be received as a candidate under the care of Classis, or be privileged to minister in, or receive a call from our churches, unless he shall have spent the same amount of time in actual attendance on theological instruction that is required from our own students; and any deficiency in this respect shall be made up by study in our own Seminary.

4. It is enjoined on the Standing Committee (on doctrine) in the several Classes, when a vacancy occurs, to send to such vacant church, immediately, a list of the licentiates of our own Seminary, and to use their endeavors to procure for them an early hearing; and it is recommended to the consistories of our churches, in all cases, promptly to endeavor to obtain their services.

5. Whenever a church becomes vacant, it shall be the duty of the Classis to exercise guardianship over it, and, when requested by the consistory, to supply it as far as practicable by their personal services—thus preventing the disorganizing influence of casual and indiscriminate ministrations; and to maintain such a supervision over it, and minister such aid as is necessary to carry out these rules, and such as a destitute church is entitled to claim from its very relations.

6. No foreign minister shall be received on mere private letters of introduction or recommendation; but, in all cases, full ecclesiastical certificates shall be required.

7. No foreign minister shall be received by any Classis, unless he shall have undergone a probation of one year under the care of a Classis, and shall then present the same testimonials, and undergo the examination, required by the first of these rules.

8. These rules shall be inserted in some conspicuous place in the minute-books of the respective Classes. Vol V., p. 387.

SEC. IV. *To appoint Committees to guard against the introduction of unsound doctrines.* Vol. I., 1815, p. 38; Vol. II., 1824, p. 47; Vol. IV., p. 293.

Resolved, That in conformity to the design of Sec. 20, Art. 1, Chap. I. of the Constitution, it is the duty of every Classis to appoint a Standing Committee, for the purpose contemplated in that section. Vol. IV., p 293.

SEC. V. *To require reports from ministers without charge.*

It is enjoined upon the several Classes to require of the ministers under their care without charges to render an account annually, at the ordinary session next preceding the meeting of General Synod, of the manner in which they have been employed the preceding year, in order that their doings may more immediately come under the review of Classis. Vol. V., p. 256.

SEC. VI. *To take measures to have the ordinances administered in vacant churches within their bounds.* Vol. I., 1817, p. 37.

SEC. VII. *Allowed to nominate members of the Board of Superintendents.*

Resolved, That instead of a Committee of Nomination, usually appointed by Synod previous to the election of the Board of Superintendents, to designate a double number from each Classis out of which the election shall be made, the respective Classes themselves shall have the right to nominate to General Synod the representatives to which they are entitled in the Board, for confirmation and appointment by Synod. Vol. IV., p. 302.

SEC. VIII. *How their nominations of members of the Board of Superintendents are to be tronsmitted to Synod.*

Resolved, That the nominations of members of the

Board of Superintendents by the several Classes, be transmitted to the General Synod by letter from the Stated Clerks of the respective Classes to the Stated Clerk of the General Syuod. Vol. IV., p. 422.

Sec. IX. *On Statistical Reports.*

Whereas, it is important that the statistical reports from our churches should be regularly made to Synod; and, whereas, some Classes have made no returns at all, and many churches have been habitually negligent in making full returns; therefore,

1. *Resolved,* That this subject be earnestly recommended to the attention of all our Classes and churches.

2. That whenever any of the churches shall be delinquent in making their statistical reports, the Classes be advised to supply such neglect, by inserting the last report from said churches, and add a note of explanation of this fact.

3. That the Stated Clerks of the several Classes be directed to send annually, a copy of their statistical reports to the Stated Clerk of General Synod. Vol. III., p. 183.

Sec. X. *Have power to decide on the validity of Romish ordination.*

Whereas, the right of ordaining the ministry of the gospel belongs to the Classes of the Church; therefore,

Resolved, That the question of the validity of Roman Catholic ordination be left to the different Classes. Vol. IV., p. 403.

Sec. XI. *Not entitled to representation in General Synod, until regularly organized.*

No Classis shall be considered as entitled to a representation in General Synod, until the same shall have been regularly organized according to the usual order, and the evidence of its organization shall have been recorded on the minutes of the Particular Synod. Vol. IV., p. 332.

SEC. XII. *Not to dissolve the pastoral relation on the ground of expediency.*

Resolved, That the resolution passed in General Synod in 1806, authorizing Classes to dissolve the connection between ministers and their congregations, on the principle of expediency, though one of the parties be averse to such dissolution, be repealed; because unconstitutional and of an evil tendency, calculated to foster strife in congregations, to encourage worldly minded professors, to excite animosities in a church against ministers, and repugnant to the practice of the Reformed Church in all ages. Vol. I., 1809, p. 18.

SEC. XIII. *May dismiss a member to an ecclesiastical body not in connection with the Reformed Church.*

The inquiry whether it be proper for Classis to give an ordained minister in our Church a dismission, to join another Church or ecclesiastical body with which the Reformed Church has no ecclesiastical intercourse or connection, was answered in the affirmative. Vol. IV., p. 322.

SEC. XIV. *To keep a lemma, entitled "Education."*

Resolved, That the several Classes be requested to place upon their order of business a lemma, entitled "Education," under which inquiries shall be instituted of each minister and elder, as to what has been done for the cause of education, and whether there are any young men within their bounds inclined to the ministry, and what means have been taken to bring the subject before them. Vol. IV., p. 504.

SEC. XV. *To keep a lemma, called "Benevolent Institutions."*

Resolved, That the different Classes be directed to have a lemma, called "Benevolent Institutions;" and that at every annual meeting of the Classes, each minister and elder shall be interrogated whether they have taken up the several collections recommended by General Synod, and make a record of the same. Vol. VI., p. 510. See, also, Vol. I., 1813, p. 30.

SEC. XVI. *To make special inquiry in relation to beneficiaries recommended by them.*

Resolved, That in all future applications for recommendations of beneficiaries, a mere examination of credentials be not deemed sufficient, and that the respective Classes be directed to inquire carefully for themselves into the talents and acquirements of the applicant, and the prospect of his becoming an acceptable and useful servant in the vineyard of our Lord Jesus Christ. Vol II., 1824, p. 54; Vol. III., p. 374; Vol. VI., p. 232.

SEC. XVII. *To inquire in relation to indigent young men desirous of entering the ministry within their bounds.*

Resolved, That it be made the duty of each Classis to inquire, at least once in every year, from the several ministers and elders composing such Classis, whether they know of any one or more persons of piety and promising talents, disposed to devote themselves to the work of the ministry, and who, being in indigent circumstances, need pecuniary assistance in prosecuting theological studies. Vol. II., Sept. 1825, p. 31.

SEC. XVIII. *To comply with the Constitution in relato the presence of Deputati at examinations.*

Resolved, That the several Classes be directed to yield a strict compliance to the rule of the Constitution in relation to the presence of a deputatus at examinations. Vol. V., p. 58.

SEC. XIX. *To give special attention to the catechetical instruction of the young.*

Whereas, it appears from the statistical tables of the different Classes, that catechetical instruction is greatly neglected in certain sections of the Church, therefore,

Resolved, That the different Classes be directed to give their special attention to this subject, so that, as far as possible, the youth in all our congregations may enjoy the benefit of pastoral catechetical instruction, according to the provisions of the standards of our Church. Vol. V., pp. 59, 60.

SEC. XX. *To become responsible for beneficiaries recommended by them.*

Resolved, That it be recommended to any Classis which may desire to aid a young man in his education for the gospel ministry, to assume the responsibility of his support, when it is at all practicable to do so. Vol VI., p. 231.

SEC. XXI. *Classis of Arcot may be represented by letter.*

Resolved, That the Classis of Arcot, in India, be authorized to represent themselves annually in this General Synod by letter. Vol. VIII., p. 609.

SEC. XXII. *Classis may express to Synod its views on acts of Synod.*

Resolved, That the Synod recognizes the unquestionable right of every Classis to express to the Synod its views of the feasibility and desirableness of every plan of Church action which the Synod may have adopted. Vol. IX., p. 39.

SEC. XXIII. *Not to examine students for licensure during the week of the meeting of the Board of Superintendents.*

Resolved, That the Synod request the various Classes not to hold their special sessions for the examination of students for licensure during the week in which the Board of Superintendents holds its annual session. Vol. IX., p. 104.

SEC. XXIV. *Reports on state of religion to contain a synopsis of statements of consistories.*

Resolved, That the several Classes * * be requested to make their reports upon the state of religion include, as far as possible, a synopsis of the statements of the individual consistories. Vol. IX., p. 154.

SEC. XXV. *To furnish consistories blank forms for statistical reports.* Vol. IX., p. 154.

SEC. XXVI. *To arrange for collection and prompt payment of apportionment for contingent expenses of Synod.*

Resolved, That it shall be the duty of each Classis to arrange for the collection and payment of the same (*i.e.* this apportionment) by its Questor at its stated fall or spring session, and to see that the amount so collected shall be punctually paid to the Treasurer of General Synod. Vol. IX., p. 212.

SEC. XXVII. *Stated Clerks to report P. O. addresses of ministers without charge.*

Resolved, That the Stated Clerks of the several Classes be directed to send up in their Statistical Reports the Post Office addresses of the members without pastoral charge. Vol. IX., p. 581.

SEC. XXVIII. *To take steps to have the claims of all the Boards presented to their churches.*

Resolved, That the Classes be urged to take such steps as shall insure that the claims of all our Boards be statedly presented to each of the churches under their care, and collections taken for them.

Resolved, That the several Classes be and are hereby requested to suggest to their churches to prepare a programme of the different objects of benevolence as recommended by the General Synod, and specify and adopt as a standing rule, certain Sabbaths when these contributions shall be annually made. Vol. X., p. 212.

SEC. XXIX. *To report names of ministers without charge, with certain notes.*

Resolved, That the Stated Clerks of the different Classes be enjoined to pay special attention to this matter in their reports, and to append to such reports the names of all ministers within their bounds, not only such as have charges, but also such as have none, and that they append also short but expressive notes to their respective name designating the positions they hold, the occupations they pursue, and the reasons of their being without a pastoral charge. Vol. XI., p. 83.

SEC. XXX. *May receive churches allowing them to retain the Scottish version of the Psalmody.*

Whereas, These churches are prevented from casting in their lot with us by reason of a partiality for the Psalmody peculiar to them; and,

Whereas, This Synod is assured of the doctrinal correctness and devotional spirit of their Psalmody; therefore,

Resolved, That in such cases, when such churches make application to be received under the care of a Classis of our Church, the said churches be allowed to retain the Psalmody, called the Scottish version, in use among them at their discretion. Vol. XI., p. 84.

SEC. XXXI. *To exercise care in recommending churches to the Board of Domestic Missions.* Vol. XI., p. 105.

SEC. XXXII. *To have the Van Benschoten Bequest read in full.*

That the reading of the said bequest by "the title" does not meet the desire of the donor, and the faith which the Church plighted to him by the acceptance of it on his terms, as appears from the terms of the document, and has been admitted by the long-established custom of our Church; and further, that it be and is hereby enjoined upon all the Classes and Synods to attend carefully to the reading of the Van Benschoten bequest at all their ordinary meetings. Vol. XI., p. 459.

SEC. XXXIII. *To provide at fall session for payment for Minutes of Synod.*

Resolved, That the Classes be directed to provide at their fall sessions for the payment for the Minutes of the General Synod, and to place the funds in the hands of their respective Questors, so that they may be paid over to the Stated Clerk of General Synod before each annual session. Vol. XI., p. 499.

SEC. XXXIV. *To endeavor to secure a due share of church contributions for our own Boards.*

Resolved, That Synod affectionately call the attention of our Classes to the small proportion of benevolent contributions given to our own Boards, as compared with the gross amount reported, and request them to use their influence as may seem to them best adapted to secure a change in this respect. Vol. XI., p. 505.

SEC. XXXV. *To spend one hour at every regular meeting in prayer and conference on benevolence.*

Resolved, That this Synod affectionately and earnestly request each Classis at every regular meeting to give at least one hour to fraternal conference and prayer with reference to the benevolent operations of the Church, that they may provoke one another to good works. Vol. XI., p. 505.

CHAPTER V.

SYNODS.

A. GENERAL SYNODS.

SEC. I. *Rules of Order*

1. At every stated meeting of the Synod, a sermon shall be preached by the last President, either before his opening the session with prayer, or at some time afterward, which the Synod shall deem most convenient.

If the last President and the Adsessor be absent, the oldest minister present shall take his place and perform the above duties.

2. The President and Adsessor shall be elected by ballot, by a majority of the members present; and if after the first vote there is no election, the choice shall be made from the two who have the highest number of votes. The clerks shall be elected by plurality.

3. The duties of the President shall be to take the chair at the hour to which the Synod stands adjourned; to open and conclude with prayer; to direct the Clerk immediately after a quorum has appeared to call the roll; to censure absentees when their absence shall be judged not to have been necessary; to propound the subjects for deliberation; to confine speakers to the point, and to save them from unnecessary interruption; to state and put the question, when the members are prepared to vote; to prevent members from leaving the Synod without permission; to decide questions of order, subject, however, to an appeal to the house by any two members; to givė the casting vote in all equal divisions; and, in general, to maintain the order and dignity becoming the judicatory of the Church of Christ.

4. After calling the roll, the minutes of the last sitting shall be read, and considered as open to correction. The business on the minutes of the last meeting or sitting, shall, without powerful reasons, be taken up and concluded first, in the order in which it stands, before any new business be introduced.

5. A motion made must be seconded, and aftewards repeated, or read aloud from the Chair, before it is debated; and every motion, except a motion for adjournment, shall be reduced to writing if any member require it.

6. An amendment may be made on any motion, and it shall be decided before the original motion. It may be, in its turn, suspended by an amendment to itself, which must first be considered and decided. But no additional amendment to an original motion can be received until the previous one has been disposed of.

7. When a question is under debate, no motion shall be received except to adjourn, to lay on the table, to postpone indefinitely, to postpone to a certain time, to commit to a standing committee, to a select one, or to the committee of the whole; to amend, or for the previous question, which motions shall have precedence in the order stated.

8. When the previous question is moved and seconded, it shall be in this form: " Shall the main question be now put?" and until it be decided all amendments and debate shall be inadmissible. If the vote be in the *affirmative*, the original motion shall be immediately put without further amendment or debate. But if there be an amendment or amendments pending at the time, the question shall first be taken on such amendment or amendments in their proper order without debate. If the vote be in the *negative* the debate shall continue as before.

9. A question shall not be called up or reconsidered at the same session of the Synod at which it was decided, unless by consent of two-thirds of the members present.

10. No member shall be allowed to protest against any of the acts of the Synod; but any member who dissents from any such acts shall have a right to require the names of all the members present, who vote for or against the same, to be entered in the minutes, and published therewith for the information of all concern-

ed. In other cases, the yeas and nays shall not be recorded unless on the demand of one-fifth of the members present.

11. The mover and seconder of a motion may withdraw it before debate has commenced on it, but not afterwards, unless by leave of Synod.

12. In filling blanks, when various motions are made, the vote shall always be first on the highest number and longest time.

13. Every member shall rise and address himself to the President only, closely attending to the subject in debate, avoiding all personal reflections; and no member, without the special permission of the Synod, shall speak more than twice on the same subject. When two or more members rise to speak at the same time, the President shall determine who of them shall be heard first.

14. After the President has begun to take the vote, or the Clerk to call the roll on a division of the house, no debate nor remark shall be allowed.

15. A motion to adjourn or to lay on the table, and all motions in relation to priority of business, shall be decided without debate. The motion to postpone or to commit shall preclude all debate of the main question.

16. When an appeal is taken from a decision of the Chair on a point of order, the President shall have the right to explain the grounds of his decision, but the appeal shall be decided by the house without debate.

17. No member shall leave the Synod to return home or for other business without their consent; nor shall members, without express permission, engage in private conversation, go from or change their seats during the transaction of business; interrupt another when he is speaking, except he be out of order, or to correct

mistakes and misrepresentations; and if any member act indecently or disorderly, contrary to these rules, the President shall reprove or otherwise censure him, as the Synod shall judge proper; the member still having the privilege, if he think himself denied of any right or unjustly blamed by the President, of respectfully and modestly requiring the decision of the house in the case.

18. All the sittings of General Synod shall be concluded by regular adjournment and prayer.

19. At the close of every session of General Synod the roll shall be called, and the names of those who are absent without permission shall be recorded.

20. *Standing Committees:*

(1.) Professorate.
(2.) Overtures.
(3.) Synodical Minutes.
(4.) Domestic Missions.
(5.) Foreign Missions.
(6.) State of Religion.
(7.) Education.
(8.) Judicial Business.
(9.) Widows' and Disabled Ministers' Funds.
(10.) Publication.
(11.) Nominations.
(12.) Correspondence.
(13.) Accounts.
(14.) Leave of Absence.

21. All distinctive titles or appendages to the names of members of Synod shall be omitted in recording the minutes of this Synod; said distinctive titles being prefixed or appended to the name of the member in the list of members constituting the Synod.

22. *Primarii and Secundi:*

(1.) When a Primarius shall find it impracticable to attend the judicatory to which he is delegated, that then it shall be his duty as soon as may be, to notify a Secundus, and that when he shall take his seat, it shall not be vacated to give place to the Primarius.

(2.) At the commencement of the session, the members delegated, whether Primarii or Secundi, shall be recognized and recorded, but when the Primarius shall appear at any subsequent period of the session, then the Primarius shall take the seat of the Secundus, and the Secundus shall not be considered a member again, unless by the request of the Primarius, and express permission obtained by the Synod.

23. *Judicial Business:*

(1.) Any appeal, complaint, or other judicial business, which shall be presented or reported to the Synod, shall be first referred, with all the papers and documents appertaining thereto, to the Committee on Judicial Business, who shall inquire whether the same has been regularly brought before the Synod, and whether all the constitutional steps in the case have been taken, and, if the same shall be found in order, they shall digest and arrange all the papers and documents connected therewith, that the subsequent proceedings in the case before the Synod may be regular and systematic; provided, nevertheless, that the said committee shall be required to report upon every matter that may be referred to them.

(2) Whenever any case thus reported shall be taken up for trial, the President shall solemnly announce from the Chair that the Synod is about to proceed to the consideration of judicial business, and enjoin on the members to recollect and regard their character as judges of

the highest court of Jesus Christ on earth, known to the Constitution of the Reformed Church; after which it shall not be in order, during the pending of such trial, to transact any legislative business bearing on the case.

(3.) In recording their decision, it shall be the duty of the court who have tried any judicial business in the original case, or by appeal, to set forth at length the reasons thereof, that the record may exhibit, as far as practicable, every thing that had an influence on their judgment; a certified copy of which, with the act of proceeding appealed from, shall be sent up by them to the court to whom the appeal may be taken. Such inferior conrt shall also be permitted to send a commissioner to the Synod, for the purpose of making any explanation relative to said case, it being expressly understood that in every case the original parties be not lost sight of in any stage of trial.

(4.) In taking up an appeal, after having ascertained that the appellant has conducted it regularly, the following shall be the order of trial:

[1.] The sentence appealed from shall be read.

[2.] The appeal and reasons of appeal shall be read.

[3.] All the documents in the case shall be read, in the order prescribed by the Committee on Judicial Business.

[4.] The original parties shall be heard, commencing with the appellant.

[5.] The commissioner of the inferior judicatory which has tried the appeal may be heard in explanation of the grounds of their decision, and of the manner of their proceeding in the case.

[6.] The appellant may be heard in reply.

(5.) After all parties shall have been fully heard, and

all the information gained by the Synod which shall be deemed necessary, the parties shall withdraw, when the roll shall be called, that every member may have an opportunity to express his opinion on the case, after which the final vote may be taken.

(6.) The decision may be either to confirm or reverse, in whole or in part, the judgment of the inferior judicatory, or to remit the cause with instructions or for a new trial.

(7.) In the trial of all judicial business brought before the Synod, by complaint or reference, the same order of proceeding shall be observed, as far as practicable, as in cases of appeal, but no complaint shall be entertained unless notice of the same shall have been given before the rising of the judicatory whose act is complained of, or within ten days thereafter.

24. *Religious Exercises :*

(1.) The afternoon of the first day shall be devoted to exercises of prayer and praise.

(2.) The first half hour of each subsequent morning session shall be so spent after the reading of the minutes.

(3.) The Lord's Supper shall be observed on the afternoon of the second day.

(4.) A sermon in behalf of the benevolent operations of the Church shall be preached on the evening of the sixth day of the session.

25. The morning of the third day of the session shall be devoted to the purpose of hearing from the Secretaries of our various Boards such oral statements as they shall see fit to make ; after which, an opportunity shall be afforded for a free interchange of opinion and feeling among the members of the Synod in regard to the benevolent operations of the Church.

26. A rule of order may be suspended for the time by unanimous consent.

27. These rules (except 22, 23, 24, and 25) shall be read at the opening of each General Synod.

SEC. II. *Its powers at a special meeting.*

The General Synod of the Reformed Church, when convened in special session by the call of the President, has full power and authority to transact generally any business within the ordinary limits of its constitutional power, whether specified in the call or not. Vol. IV., p. 9.

The same point was decided in the same way in 1804. (p. 5.)

SEC. III. *Expenses of Delegates to Synod to be paid.*

In order to avoid disappointments originating from pecuniary considerations, it is recommended to the Particular Synods to enjoin it on their respective Classes, to make suitable provision for defraying the expenses of their delegates. Vol. I., 1809, p. 17. But see 1815, p. 74.

SEC. IV. *Credentials of Delegates.*

Resolved, That the Stated Clerks of the several Particular Synods be and are hereby instructed to send the credentials of delegates to the General Synod to the said delegates, immediately upon their election, and also to the Stated Clerk of the General Synod. Vol. XI., p. 499.

SEC. V. *Directions with reference to Minutes of Synod.*

Resolved, That the Annual Reports of the several Clas ses be this year and hereafter arranged in alphabetical order, with a view to greater facility of reference; and that the initials of the Particular Synods to which they respectively belong be annexed.

Resolved, That there be published in the minutes of this Synod, this year and hereafter, the following:

1. The order of the Lemmata, to each of which shall be annexed a reference to the page of the minutes on which it may be found.

2. A list of the names of all who from the first shall have occupied the office of President of this Synod, and likewise a list of all who shall have occupied the office of Stated Clerk; and that the names of all, respectively, be preceded by the year of their election, and followed by the name of the State in which they reside, and of the place in which the meeting was held.

3. An alphabetical list of all our ministers, with their respective places of residence, or post office addresses, annexed, together with a reference to the page of the Minutes of Synod upon which each name may be found in the Classical Report. Vol. X., p. 208.

SEC. VI. *Stated clerks to have charge of accounts for the minutes.*

Resolved, That the accounts for the Minutes of the General Synod be transferred from the Treasurer to the Stated Clerk, and that he furnish the usual item on that subject for the "Annual Digest."

SEC. VII. *Salary of Treasurer.*

Resolved, That the salary of the Treasurer of General Synod shall be $1,000.

In view of the fact that the management of the Widows' Fund involves a much larger amount of labor than any other of the funds of Synod;

Resolved, That of the salary of the Treasurer, $250 shall be paid from the Widows' Fund, and the remainder apportioned among the other funds.

SEC. VIII. *Permanent Clerk appointed.*

Resolved, That the office of Permanent Clerk be restored, and that the division of labor be arranged between this officer and the Stated Clerk.

Resolved, That the Permanent Clerk be allowed a salary of fifty dollars per annum, and that his necessary expenses while attending the meetings of General Synod be paid. Vol. XI., p. 663.

B. PARTICULAR SYNODS. (See also Appendix.)

SEC. I. *To administer Lord's Supper at their meetings.*

Resolved, That it be recommended to the Particular Synods to connect with their services the administration of the Lord's Supper. Vol. VIII., p. 420.

SEC. II. *Anniversaries to be connected with them.*

Resolved, That it be recommended to the several bodies of our Church, so to arrange their anniversary celebrations as to hold them during and in connection with the regular meetings of one or more of the Particular Synods of our Church.

SEC. III. *To send transcripts of answers to second and third constitutional questions.*

Resolved, That the Particular Synod be directed to send up to General Synod a transcript of the Classical records in regard to the answers to the second and third constitutional questions proposed at the spring session of each Classis. Vol. VIII., p. 420.

SEC. IV. *To embody in reports on State of Religion extracts from the minutes of Classis.*

Resolved, That it be recommended to the Particular Synods, in preparing their reports on the State of religion, to embody in them, as far as possible, an extract from the minutes of each Classis, embracing a comparative statement of the state of religion in their bounds, as materials out of which the General Synod may form a more accurate estimate of the condition of the whole Church. Vol. VIII., p. 542.

SEC. V. *Particular Synod of Chicago organized.*

Ordered by General Synod and Committee appointed June, 1856. Committee reported the organization effected September 3, 1856. Their report was accepted and adopted June, 1857. Vol. IX., pp. 91 and 133.

SEC. VI. *To furnish Classes with blank forms for statistical reports.* Vol. IX., p. 154.

SEC. VII. *To insert in their Minutes a tabular summary of statistics.*

Resolved, That the Stated Clerks of the Particular Synods be requested to prepare, and insert in their printed Minutes, a tabular summary of the statistical tables of their respective Synods. Vol. IX., p. 296.

SEC. VIII. *Eastern Synods to visit the Western by delegates.*

Resolved, That the visitation of the Particular Synod of the West by delegates from the Particular Synods of the East meets with the decided approval of this body, Vol. X., p. 348.

SEC. IX. *Recommended to extend the time of their meetings and make some other changes.*

Resolved, That it be earnestly recommended to the Particular Synods that they extend the time of their meetings; that they cease to refer to General Synod matters which could be as well, and perhaps, on some accounts, better dealt with by themselves; that they abound more in devotional exercises, and that they endeavor to inaugurate measures which, through the blessing of God, may increase the spirituality and usefulness of pastors, elders, and church members. Vol. XI., p. 83.

SEC. X. *To send annually at least ten copies of Minutes to General Synod.* Vol. III., p. 77.

SEC. XI. *Particular Synod of New Brunswick—Committee appointed to organize.* Vol. XI., p. 631.

CHAPTER VI.

BOARDS OF THE CHURCH.

A. BOARD OF DIRECTION.

SEC. I. *The Act of Incorporation.*

Be it enacted, by the People of the State of New York, represented in the Senate and Assembly, That the General Synod of the Reformed Protestant Dutch Church shall be and hereby is declared to be a body corporate and politic, by the name and style of "The General Synod of the Reformed Protestant Dutch Church," with full power to sue and be sued, defend and be defended by that name, in all courts of law and equity; and to have a common seal, and to alter the same at pleasure;

and also to take, purchase and hold real and personal estate, and to sell and convey the same, provided the yearly value of the same shall not exceed the sum of ten thousand dollars, and that the same shall not be appropriated to any other than religious and charitable uses and purposes.

And be it further enacted, That it shall be lawful for the regular members of the said General Synod, at their stated annual meetings, to appoint a President, three Directors and a Treasurer of said corporation ; and to make and ordain by-laws and regulations relating to the management and disposition of their real and personal estate, the duties of the said President, Directors and Treasurer, and the duration of their respective offices: *Provided always*, That such by-laws and regulations shall not be inconsistent with the Constitution and Laws of this State, or of the United States.

And be it further enacted, That it shall at all times be lawful for the Legislature to repeal or amend this act. Vol. II., 1819, p. 46.

(b.) *Change made by Legislature of New York*, 1869.

The People of the State of New York, represented in Senate and Assembly. do enact as follows :

SEC. 1. It shall be lawful for the General Synod of the Reformed Protestant Dutch Church, to take and hold by gift, grant, devise or otherwise hereafter made and by purchase hereafter made, to hold and convey any estate, real or personal, provided that the clear annual value or income of such estate shall not exceed the sum of fifteen thousand dollars, exclusive of such Professorships and Scholarships for the purposes of theological education as may be from time to time endowed ; but the right herein granted to take and hold real and personal estate by bequest or devise shall be subject to all provisions of law in relation to devises and bequests by last will and testament. Nothing herein contained is to be construed to apply to any question, matter, thing involved or at issue in any action now pending in any court in which said Synod is a party, or to any action or proceeding which may hereafter be commenced against or by, or on behalf of said Synod, or in which said Synod shall be a party, and which shall not relate to property granted, bequeathed, or devised to or acquired by said Synod subsequent to the passage of this act.

SEC. 2. This act shall take effect immediately.

Passed, April 14th, 1869. Vol. XI., p. 555

SEC. II. *By-Laws.**

1. The Board shall hold a stated meeting once in every month.

2. Special meetings shall be called by the President whenever he shall deem it necessary, or by any two of the Directors.

3. A majority of the Board shall be a quorum to tran sact business, and in the absence of the President they shall have the power to elect a President, *pro tem.*

4. The Board is authorized to demand and receive all moneys belonging to the General Synod of the Reformed Church; to draw upon the Treasurer from time to time for such money in his hands as may be necessary to answer the appropriations made by the Synod, and to apply to their specific objects the benefactions of societies, congregations, and individuals. They shall, in the most advantageous manner, invest all moneys that shall come into their hands for any particular fund, and which have not been appropriated.

---

* See Appendix.

They shall appoint a Secretary, whose duty it shall be to keep their minutes, to correspond with the agents appointed by this Synod for the collecting of moneys for the use of Synod, and with agents which have been or may be appointed by other judicatories of the Church.

5. The Treasurer shall keep a regular and accurate account of all moneys by him received and disbursed, designating the specific purposes for which they have been received or expended, and shall lay before the Board such account quarterly or as often as they shall require.

6. The Board shall report annually to the General Synod a statement of the funds, with such remarks as they may think necessary.

7. The President, Directors, and Treasurer shall hold their offices for one year, or until others are appointed, except in cases of malconduct, for which the Treasurer, or any member of the Board, may be suspended and reported to the General Synod at their next meeting.

8. All drafts on the Treasurer, or orders of the Board, shall be signed by the President, who shall affix the seal of the corporation, in the presence of the Board, to such instruments of writing as may require it. Vol. II., 1819, pp. 48. 49,

SEC. III. *Enjoined to collect certain funds.*

The General Synod enjoin it on the Board of Corporation to collect all moneys due from persons who have received or may receive aid from the Theological Funds, and who have connected or may connect themselves with other denominations, within the time specified in the order of the Synod. 1820, p. 69; repeated Vol. V., p. 76.

SEC. IV. *Have power to fill vacancies in their own body.*

Resolved, That the Board of Corporation have power to fill any vacancies that may occur in the Board by death or otherwise, during the recess of General Synod. 1824, p. 55; Vol. V., p. 76. VOL. X., p. 627.

SEC. V. *Have power to manage all the property of Synod.*

Resolved, That the Board of Corporation be and hereby is empowered to take care of and manage all the property, real and personal, of General Synod, so as to preserve it from loss and injury, and increase its pro ductiveness during the pleasure of Synod. 1825, p. 40.

SEC. VI. *To use the name "Board of Direction of the Corporation."* Vol. III,, p. 69.

SEC. VII. *Have charge of the Widows' Fund.*

The fund for the relief of disabled ministers, and the widows and children of ministers, shall be administered by the Board of Corporation, during the pleasure and under the control of General Synod.

The moneys belonging to this fund shall be kept separate and distinct from all other funds belonging to General Synod.

The officers of the Board of Corporation shall be offi cers of the trust. The Treasurer's duty shall be to collect the income and to make all payments. He shall report minutely and fully to General Synod at each of its annual meetings. Vol. V., p. 111.

SEC. VIII. *To prepare the annual Digest.*

The duty of preparing an annual Digest of the pecuniary concerns of the Synod was transferred from the

Treasurer and Stated Clerk of General Synod to the Board of Corporation in 1819. Vol. II., 1819, p. 79.

SEC. IX. *Power to hold real estate in New Jersey.*

Application was made to the Legislature of the State of New Jersey for an act authorizing them to hold real property in that State, which was granted. Vol. II., 1826, p. 15.

SEC. X. *Authorized to receive the funds constituting the Scholarships.*

Resolved, That the Board of Corporation be authorized to receive from the Treasurer of the Board of Education the funds constituting the scholarships, and that the proceeds of the same, together with those of the Heyer scholarship, be applied under the direction of the Board of Education. Vol. IV., p. 320.

SEC. XI. *Authorized to receive deeds for Rutgers College.* 1823, p, 53; 1824, p. 54; 1825, p. 9; 1826, p. 15; 1827, p. 19.

SEC. XII. *Authorized to execute certain leases to Rutgers College.* Vol. IV., p. 509; Vol. V., p. 436; Vol. VI., p. 9.

SEC. XIII. *To require a list of the securities for loans made from the Van Benschoten Fund.*

Resolved, That in future the Board of Direction require from the Board of Trustees of Rutgers College a list of the securities for the loans made of moneys belonging to the Van Benschoten and Knox Funds, to be transmitted to Synod. Vol. VI., p. 243.

SEC. XIV. *To pay expenses of President to open Synod.*

Resolved, That the Treasurer of General Synod be authorized to pay the necessary travelling expenses of the President of the former Synod when he attends to open the Synod, and is not a delegate to Synod. Vol. VIII., p. 376.

SEC. XV. *To borrow money when necessary to pay salaries.*

Resolved, That the Board of Direction be authorized to borrow on the credit of the General Synod, from time to time, such sum or sums of money as may be necessary to pay the salaries of the Professors, and of the employees of the General Synod, as the same shall become due. Vol. XI., p. 189.

SEC. XVI. *To hold property in Michigan.*

Application was made to the Legislature of Michigan for an act authorizing them to hold property in that State, which was granted. Vol. X., p. 253.

B. BOARD OF DOMESTIC MISSIONS.

SEC. I. *Plan adopted by General Synod.*

1. That the Board of Domestic Missions hereafter consist of twenty-four members, one-half of whom shall reside in the cities of New York, Brooklyn, and Jersey City, the residue to be appointed from other parts of the Church—one third of the number to be elected annually by General Synod.

2. That the Board shall meet on the second Tuesday after the adjournment of General Synod—on the Tuesday after the meeting of the Executive Committee in November, and on the Tuesday after the meeting of the said committee in April.

3. That the first meeting of this Board shall be held on the second Tuesday of November next, at the Con-

sistory Room in Fulton street, New York, at 10 o'clock, A. M.; and that at such meeting, in addition to the organization of the Board, they shall divide themselves into three classes; and that their subsequent meetings be held at such hour as they may themselves decide, and that the old Board continue to act in the meantime.

4. That at these meetings of the Board all the actions of the Executive Committee shall be revised and passed upon; and that at each meeting the Treasurer shall make a report of the state of the funds.

5. That said Board shall annually elect an Executive Committee, consisting of nine members, to manage the Missionary and Church Extension concerns, of which the Corresponding Secretary and Treasurer shall be ex-officio members; of the remaining seven, *three* shall be laymen and *four* ministers; that *five* members of said Committee shall form a quorum for the transaction of business, and that they meet monthly.

6. That the churches be earnestly recommended to make annual collections for the purpose of aiding feeble churches in erecting houses of worship, and that the several Classes be directed to see that this recommendation be attended to in the best manner to accomplish the object.

7. That authority to act upon the principle of Church extension, in aiding feeble congregations to erect houses of worship, be added to the existing powers of the Board of Domestic Missions; and that all moneys collected under the authority of Synod for such purpose be committed to the said Board for distribution under the distinct injunction that the exercise of the charity be restricted to cases of urgency, where due economy and modesty shall have marked the plan of structure and rate of ex-

penditure; where the congregation applying for help, pledge themselves for the speedy completion of the building without leaving debt, and where legal obligations be entered into that the sum granted shall be returned to the Reformed Church, in case of the enterprise failing, or the alienation of the property from a sacred use or the authority of our denomination.

8. That except when otherwise ordered by the donors or testators, all moneys collected for Church Extension shall be distributed freely, as cases of need occur, that the liberality of the Church be promptly as well as wisely applied.

9. That the Board of Domestic Missions be requested to devise and endeavor to establish an efficient system for the collection of funds, by which, so far as possible, burdens may be equalized, attention to the charities of the Church kept up, and regularity and increase of contribution secured; that the action of the Board may be more confident, because more assured of funds, and the great advantages of general, systematic liberality gained and maintained.

10. That all other enactments touching the powers and other matters that relate to the Constitution of the Board, shall remain in full force.

SEC. II. *Not to make appropriations in certain cases.*

The Board of Missions is instructed not to make appropriations in behalf of any person laboring in any vacancy within our bounds, unless he shall have been regularly licensed to preach the gospel, and only then, when the established rules of the Board shall have been complied with. Vol. V., p. 59.

SEC. III. *To organize vacant Churches through Classis.*

The Board of Missions shall direct their missionaries,

whenever a church is to be organized as the result of their labors, that application be made to the next contiguous Classis for their action upon the case, that the organization may be effected in strict accordance with the Constitution. Vol. V., p. 294.

SEC. IV. *Not to aid a Church unless it be recommended by the Classis to which it belongs.*

Resolved, That the Board of Domestic Missions should make no appropriation to any church asking aid in the settlement of a pastor, unless they have before them a recommendation of the application of such church from the Classis within whose bounds it is located. Vol. VII., 1846, p. 89.

SEC. V. *Have power to appoint Commissioners.*

Resolved, That the power of the Board of Domestic Missions to appoint commissioners from time to time, as they may deem necessary for the furtherance of the work committed to their trust, be, and hereby is, recognized on the part of the Synod. Vol. VII., 1846, p. 88.

SEC. VI. *Are authorized to fund legacies.*

Resolved, That the Board of Domestic Missions are authorized to fund any moneys accruing from bequests, and expend only the proceeds of the same, as their circumstances may from time to require. Vol. VII., 1846, p. 89.

SEC. VII. *Not to interfere with ecclesiastical judicatories.*

Resolved, That this Synod cannot approve of any interference of their Missionary Boards with their ecclesiastical judicatories, and that the respective Boards of

Missions be enjoined to refrain from any such interference. Vol. III., p. 298.

SEC. VIII. *Who may be honorary members, and their privileges.*

Any person contributing $30 at one time may be an honorary member, but without any privilege of deliberating or voting. Vol. IV., p. 234. This sum was subsequently increased to $50. Vol. V., p. 85.

SEC. IX. *Candidates or ministers of other denominations not to be employed as missionaries.*

Whereas, it appears from the minutes of the Committee on Missions, that an engagement had been entered into with a licentiate not belonging to our communion, employing him as a missionary; it is hereby

Resolved, As the sense of General Synod, that the Committee of Missions consider themselves to be hereafter restricted in their choice of missionaries to the ministers and candidates of the Reformed Church. 1812, p. 32.

SEC. X. *To apply to the Stated Clerks of Classes for information.*

Resolved, That hereafter, in every case where the Board deem it necessary to have additional information of the state and abilities of the churches applying for aid, the Board shall apply to the Stated Clerks of the respective Classes, whose duty it shall be to furnish detailed facts and information to the Board. Vol. VII., p. 195.

SEC. XI. *Method of establishing missions advised.*

Whereas, it is desirable that the operations of our Church, in extending its growth at the West, be conducted in the most earnest and efficient manner, especially at the present opportunity; therefore,

Resolved, That this Synod respectfully suggest to the Board of Domestic Missions the following method, as, in our view, best calculated to promote the end:

Let the Board at once select and appoint at least four or five missionaries, partly from those who have already had some experience in the ministry, to be sent out in company to neighboring places in some portion of the West, as yet unoccupied by our Church, but adjoining the present Classes, the distinct duty of such missionaries being to establish a new Classis as soon as three churches may have been organized. Vol. X., p. 493.

SEC. XII. *Corresponding Secretary to visit the West annually.*

Resolved, That in our judgment an annual official visit to the West, by the Corresponding Secretary, would be so beneficial to all the interests involved as fully to justify the needful time and expenditure. Vol. X., p. 493.

SEC. XIII. *To secure* $50,000 *for a Church Building Fund.*

Resolved, That the Board be authorized to take such measures as it may deem expedient to secure at as early a day as practicable an endowment of the Church Building Fund to an amount of not less than $50,000. Vol. X., p. 640.

SEC. XIV. *To endeavor to enlist in its service prominent and able men.*

Resolved, That the Board endeavor to enlist prominent and able men for this service, and send them forth to the work as soon as practicable. Vol. X., p. 639.

SEC. XV. *Not to encroach on ground occupied by the Presbyterian Church.*

Resolved, That we enjoin upon our Board of Domestic Missions to avoid encroaching upon the ground occupied by the congregations of the Presbyterian Church. Vol. XI., p. 43.

C. BOARD OF FOREIGN MISSIONS.

SEC. I. *Plan adopted by General Synod.*

CONSTITUTION.

Art. 1. The management and control of the Foreign Missions of the Reformed Church, as well as the institution of new Missions, and the appointment of Missionaries, shall be committed to the BOARD OF FOREIGN MISSIONS, subject to the revision and instruction of the General Synod.

Art. 2. This Board shall not be restricted in the sending of Missionaries to any part of the world, or to any class of persons who are without a pure Gospel, when Divine Providence opens the way to them, and the men and means are furnished.

Art. 3. The Board of Foreign Missions shall consist of twenty-four members, (of whom one-third shall be chosen at each annual meeting of the General Synod), with the Corresponding Secretary and Treasurer, who shall be *ex-officio* members.

Art. 4. The Board of Foreign Missions shall hold its first meeting each year, as soon as practicable after the meeting of the General Synod, at which the officers for the year shall be chosen.

Art. 5. The Board of Foreign Missions shall have authority to employ ordained Ministers, and Licentiates, the wife of each of whom shall be regarded as an Assistant Missionary; Physicians, Colporteurs, Printers, unmarried Female Teachers, all to be at the time of appointment members in communion with the Reformed Church, or, having taken the measures necessary to become such—and all proper agencies for raising means in our Churches for the support of the Missions, and the use of the Press, both at home and abroad.

Art. 6. Any person by the contribution of Fifty Dollars at one time, may become a member for life of the Board of Foreign Missions, and shall have the privilege of meeting with the Board, and participating in its deliberations, without being entitled to vote.

Art. 7. The Board of Foreign Missions shall submit to the General Synod, at each annual meeting, a faithful report of its acts, with the annual account of the Treasurer, properly audited, and submit for approval such plans and measures as may require the specific attention of the General Synod. The Corresponding Secretary shall be present at each meeting of Synod, to make such explanations as may be called for.

Art. 8. It shall be the steady aim of the Board of Foreign Missions to secure as early as may be wise, the organization by the Missionaries of Churches, Classes, and other Church Courts, according to the order of the Reformed Church.

Art. 9. The Board of Foreign Missions shall meet at least quarterly, at such hour and place as it may itself agree on, and when convened, seven members shall constitute a quorum.

Art. 10. The Board shall have power to fill vacancies, which may occur in the progress of the year—the persons chosen to hold such place until the next meeting of the General Synod.

Art. 11. Extra meetings of the Board may be called on the vote of the Executive Committee, or the written request of any three members.

Resolved, That the Synod hereby approve and sanction * * * the Constitution * * * as of late adopted by the Board of Foreign Missions. Vol. IX., p. 263.

SEC. II. *Corresponding Secretary to present the claims of the foreign field to students.*

Resolved, That the Corresponding Secretary of our Board be requested to present the claims of the foreign field to the students of our Seminary as often during each year as he may find it convenient. Vol. IX., p. 225.

SEC. III. *Authorized to apply for an act of incorporation.*

Resolved, That the Board of Foreign Missions * * be and hereby is authorized to apply to the Legislature of this (New York) State for an act of incorporation. Vol. IX., p. 458.

SEC. IV. *Authorized to open a credit of* £8,000 *sterling for operations abroad.*

Resolved, That the General Synod approve of the opening of a credit by their Board of Foreign Missions to the amount of £8,000 sterling, for the purpose of carrying on their Missionary operations abroad. Vol. IX., p. 635.

D. BOARD OF EDUCATION.

SEC. I. *Plan adopted by General Synod.*

The Board of Education shall consist of 24 members,

to be elected for three years, of whom nine shall constitute a quorum for the transaction of business. They shall be divided into three classes, one of which shall be elected annually. They shall have power to choose their own officers, and shall have the immediate care of all the beneficiaries and education interests of General Synod, including such beneficiaries as shall receive support or assistance from the Van Benschoten and Knox Funds in the hands of the Trustees of Rutgers College, and shall have power to make such By-Laws as they may deem necessary, and as shall not contravene the rules established by General Synod, and shall annually report all their proceedings to the General Synod.

MODE OF RECEPTION.

1. Every person applying to be received as a beneficiary, must be a member in regular and good standing in the Reformed Church, and must also have been a member of some Protestant Church for at least one year previous to his making such application.

2. If any one wishes to avail himself of the aid of the Church, he shall make known his desire to his Pastor, or some member of the Classis with which his church is connected, who, if he approves of it, shall make application to the Classis for his examination.

3. The examination shall be on his personal piety, on his motives for seeking the holy office of the Ministry, on his general habits, on his studies, his talents, his ability for public speaking, his health, his freedom from debt, and the necessity of his receiving aid.

4. If this examination be sustained, and Classis decide to recommend him to the Board, it shall be done in the following form :

At a meeting of the Classis of , held at , on the day of , 18 , the person whose name is given in the following report, having been examined in conformity with the Plan of Education adopted by General Synod, is hereby recom mended to receive aid from the Educational Funds of the Church :

REPORT.

Name	Age	Residence	With what Church connected	State of Education	Lowest amount required	Health	Debts

5. When the beneficiary thus recommended shall have been received by the Board of Education, his name shall be entered upon a book kept by the Secretary, and ruled in the following manner :

No.	Name	Age	Residence	With what Church connected	State of Education	Place of Study	Lowest amount required	When received	When his connection ceased	General Remarks

6. This power of examining candidates shall be vested in the Board of Education also, and they shall be em-

powered to make such examination whenever in their judgment they may deem it necessary or desirable.

7. Every beneficiary shall have finished a complete and regular course of Collegiate study before he shall be allowed to enter the Theological Seminary, unless a dispensation shall have been obtained from General Synod.

8. If at any time there shall have been discovered in any student such defect in capacity, diligence, prudence or piety, as would render his introdnction into the Ministry a doubtful measure, it shall be considered the sacred duty of the Board to withdraw their appropriations.

Students shall also cease to receive the assistance of the Board when their health shall have become such as to unfit them for study, and for the work of the ministry; when they are manifestly improvident, and contract debts without reasonable prospects of payment: when they marry, and when they receive the assistance of any other Educational Board or Society.

9. If any student fail to continue in his preparations for the work of the ministry, unless in the judgment of the Board he be providentially prevented, or if he cease to be in connection with the Reformed Church, or if the withdrawal of his support shall have been rendered necessary by wilful neglect of duty or mal-conduct, he shall be required, at the discretion of the Executive Committee of the Board, to refund all the money which he may have received from the Board.

10. When any student shall have found it necessary to relinquish study for a time, to teach or otherwise increase the means of support, he shall first obtain the consent of the Executive Committee, and it shall be left to their decision whether his appropriation, under the

circumstances, shall be continued, or continued only in part.

11. All the instructors of the young men under the care of this Board shall be furnished with forms of a report, and shall be requested to fill up and forward the same to the Secretary of the Board, at the close of each current term of study.

12. All the students shall be considered to be under the Pastoral care of the Secretary, who shall endeavor to cultivate a friendly intercourse with them, and, if he deem it advisable, occasionally to address them individually or together.

13. All previous action of General Synod which is in conflict with the Plan of the Board of Education now adopted, is hereby repealed. Vol. IX., pp. 198, 200.

SEC. II. *To bestow $30 on each beneficiary on completing his Theological course.*

Resolved, That the Board of Education bestow the sum of thirty dollars, * * * on each beneficiary, if asked for, at the completion of his theological course. Vol. VIII., p. 457.

SEC. III. *To accept two years' Domestic Missionary service in lieu of repayment.*

Resolved, That the Board of Education be directed to accept from all beneficiaries, after their licensure, two years' service under the care of the Board of Domestic Missions, as a full satisfaction for all aid afforded them by the Board of Education. Vol. VIII., p. 457.

SEC. IV. *Empowered to appoint a Corresponding Secretary.*

Resolved, That the Board of Education, be and they

are hereby empowered to appoint a Corresponding Secretary * * *, who shall be devoted to the advancement of the educational interests of our Church. Vol. VIII.. p. 461; Vol. IX., page 17.

SEC. V. *Appropriations raised to* $150 *per annum.*

Resolved, That the Board of Education be instructed to add thirty dollars per annum to the sum of $120 heretofore granted to the beneficiaries * * in our Institutions at New Brunswick. Vol. VIII., p. 464.

SEC. VI. *To fix amount of Secretary's salary.*

Resolved, That the General Synod remove the limit of the amount which the Board may pay to the Secretary, leaving the amount of his salary to be determined by the Board. Vol. IX., p. 197.

SEC. VII. *To record terms of bequests in a suitable book.*

Resolved, That the Board of Education cause to be procured, and recorded in a book provided for the purpose, a transcript of the bequests or grants made, that the specific terms of each may be sacredly observed in all particulars expressed therein. Vol. VIII., p. 467.

SEC. VIII. *To fill vacancies occurring between meetings of Synod.*

Resolved, That the Board of Education be authorized to fill any vacancies that may occur in their number between the sessions of General Synod; and that the persons so chosen shall serve till the expiration of the time of those whose places they take. Vol. IX., p. 197.

SEC. IX. *Classis or Church in recommending a beneficiary to make efforts to sustain him.*

It is recommended to any Classis which may desire

to aid a young man in his education for the gospel ministry, to assume the responsibility of his support, when it is at all practicable to do so.

When any church recommends a beneficiary to the funds of the Education Board, or any other funds at the disposal of this Synod for classical or theological education, such church or consistory shall first make an effort to sustain such young man, and report to the Classis with which such church is connected to what extent they shall be able to assist. Vol. VI., p. 231.

SEC. X. *The Board to seek repayment in certain cases.*

The Board shall observe all such young men as may abandon the prosecution of their preparation for the ministry, or may retire to some other denomination, and demand from them the repayment of what they have received, and that in case of their failing to do so without satisfactory reasons, their names be published by the Board. Vol. V., p. 393.

SEC. XI. *Beneficiaries must be poor.*

In order to prevent application for aid on the part of those whose parents are able to support them, the Board of Superintendents is directed to appropriate no moneys to any student who has not a certificate from the consistory of the church to which he belongs, that his parents are unable or unwilling to support him, or that he has not sufficient means of support. Vol. II., 1819, p. 40.

SEC. XII. *Great care to be exercised in receiving beneficiaries.*

Resolved, That the several Classes be and hereby are solemnly and urgently urged to exercise great care in their proposed examination of beneficiaries; and that they be and hereby are enjoined to require clear evidence, not only of piety and prudence, but of a high and suitable order of talent.

Resolved, That when applicants are thus recommended to the Board of Education, the Board shall also subject them to a still further examination, and shall keep a careful minute of the result, and no applicant shall be received as a beneficiary until both examinations shall have been satisfactorily sustained. Vol. VII., 1846, p. 72.

SEC. XIII. *Rights and duties of Classes, &c., in relation to beneficiaries of.*

Resolved, That all the beneficiaries supported by a Classis, a Consistory, or an Association, be put under the care of the Board of Education.

Resolved, That the Board of Education be authorized to recognize the right of Classes and Consistories and Associations to nominate beneficiaries, when accompanied with a promise to provide the means of support. Vol. IV., p. 298.

SEC. XIV. *Their beneficiaries not to be confined to any particular literary institution.*

Resolved, That the Board of Education have discretionary power in appropriating moneys in aid of our young men pursuing preparatory literary studies, in any literary institution which such Board may approve. Vol. IV., p. 516.

SEC. XV. *Names of beneficiaries not to be published.*

Resolved, That hereafter the names of beneficiaries shall not be published on the Minutes of the Particular or General Synods, and that the Stated Clerks of the respective Classes, whenever young men are recommended for aid, send a properly certified copy of such action directly to the Stated Clerk of General Synod. Vol. VII., p. 74.

SEC. XVI. *Enlargement of its powers to assist in establishment of Academies.*

Resolved, That this General Synod empower the Board of Education so to enlarge its sphere of action as to be able to coöperate efficiently and in such manner and to such extent, as in its judgment shall be wisest and best, with the various Classes in the establishment of academies and classical schools within the bounds of said Classes. Vol. X., p. 622.

E. BOARD OF PUBLICATION.

SEC. I. *Publication Committee and Lemma ordered.*

Resolved, That another committee be added to the Standing Committees to be called the "Committee on Publication," and also another lemma to be called "Board of Publication." Vol. VIII., p, 495.

SEC. II. *Plan adopted by Synod.*

CONSTITUTION.

Art. 1. The General Synod shall superintend and conduct, by its own authority, the publication and circulation of all the religious works which are designed for general diffusion among the churches under its care. The immediate care and superintendence of this work shall be entrusted to a Board appointed for that purpose. to be called the Board of Publication of the Reformed Church. Said Board to be directly amenable to the General Synod.

Art. 2, § 1. The General Synod shall, at its present session, elect twelve ministers and twelve laymen, as members of the Board of Publication; one third part of whom shall be elected annually by General Synod. These twelve ministers and twelve laymen, so appointed, shall constitute a Board, to whom shall be entrusted with such directions as may, from time to time, be given by General Synod, the superintendence of all the publications of the Reformed Church, and the circulation of such works pertaining to the History, Government, Doctrines, and Religious Literature of said Church, and of other evangelical denominations, as shall be properly approved.

§ 2. The Board shall annually report to the General Synod their proceedings, and submit, for its approval, such plans and measures as shall be deemed useful and necessary.

Art. III, § 1. The Board thus constituted, shall hold its first meeting in the Consistory Room of the North Dutch Church, in Fulton street, New York, on the last Monday of June, at 2 o'clock, P. M. At this meeting they shall divide themselves into three classes; the *first* class shall serve for *one* year, the *second* for two years, and the *third* for three years. They shall also elect a President, Vice President, Corresponding Secretary, a Treasurer, and Executive Committee to serve for the ensuing year.

§ 2. It shall belong to the Board to review and decide upon all the proceedings of the Executive Committee; to receive and dispose of their Annual Report, and present any statement of their proceedings to the General Synod which they may deem necessary.

§ 3, Seven members shall constitute a quorum for the transaction of business.

Art. IV., § 1. The Executive Committee shall consist of nine members, of which the Corresponding Secretary and Treasurer shall be *ex-officio* members; of the remaining seven, three shall be ministers and four laymen.

§ 2. The duty of the Executive Committee shall be to select and prepare suitable tracts and books for publication; to superintend and direct their distribution; to receive the reports of the Corresponding Secretary, and give him needful directions in reference to matters of business and correspondence entrusted to him; to authorize all appropriations of moneys; and to take particular direction and management of the whole subject of publication—subject, however, to the control and direction of the Board of Managers.

§ 3. The Committee shall have power to fill their own vacancies, if any occur during the recess of the Board.

Art. V. For the more permanent and efficient management of the publishing and fiscal affairs of the Board, the necessary steps shall be taken by the Board to secure an act of incorporation, under the style and title of "The Board of Publication of the Reformed Church in America."

Art. VI. The seat of operations of the Board shall be in the City of New York; but the Board shall have the power to locate Branch Depositories at any other place which they may deem expedient.

Art. VII. The financial operations of the Board shall in all cases, be conducted on the cash principle.

Art. VIII. The General Synod shall alone have power to alter, amend, or repeal any of the Articles of this Constitution. Vol. VIII., pp. 489–90.

SEC. III. *Church Schools to use their books.*

Resolved, That all the schools of the Church Parochial and Sabbath, be earnestly recommended to adopt this series (*i. e.* the Christian School Books) as a part of their course of instruction. Vol. IX., p. 334.

SEC. IV. *Issuing the Psalmody committed to them.*

Resolved, That the future issuing of our Psalmody be committed to the Board of Publication.

Resolved, That the particular attention of the Board be called to the execution of this important work, especially so far as the paper, type and binding are concerned.

Resolved, That the Board be directed to furnish our Psalm and Hymn Book to the public at cost, or as near it as possible.

Resolved, That no edition be issued unaccompanied by the doctrinal standards and liturgy of the Church. Vol. IX., p. 360.

SEC. V. *Authorized to print the Liturgy in German.*

Resolved, That the petition for the printing of the Liturgy * * * in German, for the benefit of the German brethren in our churches, be referred to the Board of Publication, with authority to so publish, if it appears best. Vol. X., p. 647.

F. VARIOUS MATTERS CONCERNING THE BOARDS.

SEC. 1. *Recommendations of Synod not intended to impose imperative obligations.*

Resolved, That this Synod, in the formation of its

Boards, and its recommendation of various charities to the several churches under its care, has never claimed to impose upon the churches, and the Classes in which they are embraced, an imperative obligation to contribute to such causes. Vol. IX., p. 38.

SEC. II. *Corresponding Secretary and Treasurer of each Board are ex-officio members of said Boards.* Vol. IX., p. 244.

SEC. III. *Names of officers and members of Boards to be published in Minutes of Synod.* Vol. IX., p. 465.

SEC. IV. *Financial year to end April* 30.

Resolved, That the financial year of the Board of Direction, and of the several other Boards under the charge of the Synod, terminate with the 30th of April of each year, and that the Treasurers make up their yearly accounts accordingly. Vol. IX., p. 465.

SEC. V. *Places of members absent continuously, one year, to be considered vacant, and filled.*

Resolved, That in all cases where a member of any one of our benevolent Boards shall fail to attend the stated meetings of such Board for a twelvemonth, continuously, such failure shall be deemed a resignation of his office, and the Board shall have liberty to fill his place by a new appointment for the unexpired term. Vol. IX., p. 582.

SEC. VI. *Reports to be printed by the opening of Synod.*

Resolved, That the various Boards of our Church be requested, if practicable, to have their reports printed and ready for distribution at the opening of the meetings of Synod. Vol IX., p. 582.

SEC. VII. *Reports to be done up with the Minutes of Synod.*

Resolved, That the Reports of each of our Boards, when printed, be done up with the Minutes of Synod, and thus distributed through the churches. Vol. X., p. 345.

SEC. VIII. *Pastors and Consistories to try to raise the standard of beneficence.*

Resolved, That it be enjoined upon pastors and consistories of churches to give increased attention to this grace, in which they ought to abound; that all proper efforts should be promptly, systematically and perseveringly made to raise the actual beneficence of all the churches to the scriptural standard. Vol IX., p. 572.

SEC. IX. *Tabular statement of receipts to be put in Minutes of Synod.*

Resolved, That the Stated Clerk of the Synod, with the aid of the Treasurers of the Boards. be requested to prepare, annually, a tabular statement of the contributions made by the several churches to the Boards, and Funds recommended by Synod; that each amount so credited shall embrace in one sum all that may have been contributed to such object, from whatever source, and that such statement be reported annually to Synod and published in the proceedings of Synod under the head of article 22d. Vol. X., p. 212.

SEC. X. *Disposition of moneys collected for Sabbath School purposes.*

Resolved, That it be recommended that of the moneys collected for Sabbath schools, those designed for their establishment and maintenance, be placed in the hands of the Treasurer of the Domestic Board, and those collected for libraries and books to be used by the schools, be placed in the hands of the Treasurer of the Board of Publication. Vol. X., p. 316.

SEC. XI. *Pulpit should teach and youth be trained to systematic benevolence.*

Resolved, That the practice of systematic benevolence is an important part of the early training of youth, and should be especially inculcated from the pulpit as one of the best exponents of Christian character. Vol. X., p. 636.

SEC. XII. *Secretaries to report Churches and pastors neglecting to aid their Boards.*

Resolved, That the Secretaries of the benevolent Boards of this Church be directed to report to General Synod, each year, the names of all churches, with the names of the pastors, that have not contributed to the funds of their respective Boards for two years consecutively. Vol. XI., p. 501.

CHAPTER VII.

EDUCATIONAL INSTITUTIONS.

A. THEOLOGICAL SEMINARY AT NEW BRUNSWICK.

SEC. I. *Plan of the School.*

ART. I. OF GENERAL SYNOD.

1. All the authority of the Reformed Church is vested in the General Synod, as the last resort. This Synod shall have paramount authority over the Theological School, its officers, laws and instructions.

2. The General Synod shall appoint a Board of Superintendents, consisting of one member from each Classis, and the respective Classes themselves shall have the right to nominate to General Synod the representatives to which they are entitled in the Board, for the confirmation and appointment by Synod. The members shall serve for three years. Those now chosen shall arrange themselves by lot into three classes; the first to serve for one year, the second for two years, the third for three years; and the Board shall report annually what seats become vacant each year. Vol. IV., p. 302; Vol. V., p. 518.

3. All the Professors of this Theological School shall be chosen by the General Synod, but in the recess of Synod the Board of Superintendents may temporarily employ a person or persons to perform the duties of a Professor.

Art. II. *Of the Superintendents.*

1. The Board of Superintendents shall meet annually in the Professoral Hall on the Tuesday preceding the third Tuesday in May, of which meeting the Stated Clerk of the Board shall give notice, through the *Christian Intelligencer*, each year; and any six members, when regularly convened, shall be a quorum for the transaction of bnsiness.

2. The Board shall open and close all their meetings with prayer.

3. The Board shall choose a President and Secretary, keep minutes of all their transactions, and lay them, with a summary account of the state of the School, before General Synod, at every stated meeting. The Stated Clerk of the Board shall be a permanent officer, *i. e.*, shall continue from year to year until he shall re-

sign, or any Board, for sufficient cause, shall elect a successor. Vol. V., p. 518.

4. The power of admitting students into the Theological School, and of granting full dismissions from the same, is vested in the Board of Superintendents; and they are directed to appoint a committee in the neighborhood of New Brunswick to act on these subjects during the recess of the Board.

5. The Board shall superintend an annual examination of all the students under the care of the Professors, to ascertain their talents and proficiency.

6. The Board shall be competent to reprimand or remove immoral or incompetent students, to inspect the doctrines taught by Professors and the general course of study, and to recommend to Synod such measures or changes as they may think advantageous to the School and the general interests of the Church.

7. The President is authorized to call a special meeting of the Board at the request of a Professor or Professors, or of any two members, at any time, provided four weeks' previous notice be given.

ART. III. *Of the Professors.*

1. The number of the Professors in the School shall be determined by General Synod, and their duties shall be prescribed by Synod, or by the person or persons who may endow a professorship, under the immediate direction of the Superintendents: *Provided,* always, that the School be not considered as completely organized without three Professors, and that all of them be ordained ministers of the Reformed Church.

2. The salaries of all the Professors hereafter appointed shall be fixed by a vote of General Synod.

3. The Professors shall attend three lectures or recitations every week, and accompany them with prayer.

4. Every Professor intending to resign, shall give six months' notice to the Board of Superintendents.

5. They shall attend morning and evening prayers with their pupils, either separately or in conjunction with the Faculty and students of Rutgers College, and supply them with the preaching of the gospel, and the administration of the sacraments by themselves or by some church in New Brunswick.

6. The Professors shall have the power of reprimanding or suspending from the School, disrespectful, immoral or incompetent students, during the recess of the Board of Superintendents, subject to the revision of the Board.

7. In respect to absences caused by sickness or pecuniary considerations, it is left to the Faculty to determine how long and for what cause a student may be absent, and yet resume his place in his class, subject to the revision of the Board. Vol. VI., p. 291.

8. The Synod will always feel gratified by enjoying the attendance of the Professors in the Theological Seminary at the sessions of Synod, whenever their professional duties will admit. 1824, p. 55; Vol. V., p. 78.

9. The Professors shall be organized into a Faculty for the exercise of the powers vested in them by this plan, and they are directed to hold monthly meetings, and more frequently if they deem it necessary. The Professors shall preside quarterly in rotation, beginning with the senior Professor. Vol. V., pp. 424, 425.

ART. IV. *Of Students.*

1. Every student before his admission to the Theological School, shall produce a certificate of his mem-

bership in some regular Protestant church, and a diploma from some literary college, or testimonials of such literary attainments as would entitle him to such diploma. He shall moreover submit to an examination by the Board, or such committee as they may appoint, of his piety, talents and such other qualifications as would give *reasonable* ground to hope that he is called of God to preach the gospel.

2. Every student in the Reformed Church shall, previous to his commencing the study of theology, make himself known as such to the Board of Superintendents, and shall be considered under the care of said Board. And every student of divinity, under whomsoever he may have studied, shall, previous to his examination by the Professor, apply for the said purpose to the Board of Superintendents, before he is examined and licensed.

3. The students shall exhibit to the Professors weekly, in rotation, one lecture or sermon on such subjects as the Professors shall appoint. and each one annually to the Superintendents, and write upon such subjects as the Professors may prescribe.

4. Strict morality, piety, diligence in studies and attendance upon lectures, recitations and prayers are required, under pain of reproof or expulsion.

5. Every student shall spend a portion of his time, morning and evening, in private devotion, and every Lord's day in public, social and private worship, with a particular reference to personal religion and growth in grace.

6. Those students who are not able to defray the expenses of their education, shall be assisted as far as practicable from the funds devoted to that purpose.

ART. 5. *Of the Time and Course of Study,*

1. The time and course of study in this School shall not be less than three years.

2. The whole course of instruction shall consist of Natural, Didactic, Polemic and Practical Theology; Biblical Literature, including Critica Sacra, Hermeneutica Sacra, Biblical Antiquities, Sacred Geography, and the Original Languages; Ecclesiastical History, including Chronology, Church Government and Pastoral Theology.

The studies of the first year, or Junior Class, shall be Critica Sacra, Biblical Antiquities, Sacred Geography, Composition, the Original Languages, the History of the Old Testament, and so much of Pastoral Theology as relates to the composition and delivery of sermons.

The studies of the second year shall be Didactic and Polemic Theology, Hermeneutica Sacra, Ecclesi astical History, and the Original Languages continued.

The studies of the third year shall be Didactic and Polemic Theology, Pastoral Theology, Ecclesiastical History, Church Government, Hermeneutica Sacra, and the Original Languages.

A general revision of the former studies shall be required at the close of each year; and there shall be anniversary exercises, in which each member of the Senior Class shall bear a part, under the direction of the Professors.

3. Students, at the expiration of three years of regular study, shall be admitted to an examination, to be conducted by the Professors before the Board of Superintendents, and, as the case may require, be con-

tinued longer in the School or furnished with a certificate signed by the Professor, which shall admit them to an examination for licensure before their respective Classes.

ART. VI. *Course in the Didactic Department.*

1. While the present text-book (Mark's Medulla) shall be put into the hands of the students, and they shall be required habitually to refer to it on the subjects of the course, as they occur, it shall be chiefly used by the Professor as his guide in the order of his instruction. But the students shall not be required either to commit to memory or to recite the same in the lecture-room. A general syllabus, however, of the whole subject, in as condensed a form as its completeness will allow, embracing definitions and the *Classis argumentorum,* drawn from the text-book by the Professor, should be in the hands of every student and committed to memory carefully by the Junior Class, to be reviewed from time to time by all the Classes.

2. The Professor shall deliver original, full, connected, continuous and well-digested written lectures upon the branches of Theological Science, in the order prescribed in the present text-book used in the Institution, and embracing a special reference to the canons and the other standards of the Church, and all the modern controversies in theology.

3. It shall be the duty of the Didactic Professor to institute and prosecute a course of elementary instruction upon the subjects of theology with the first or Junior Class, regulated by the standards of the Church, in such way as shall prepare them to enter upon the full study of the system of Didactic Theology in the second year of their course, during which year his

lectures on Didactic Theology shall be delivered. And when the students shall arrive at the third or Senior year, the Professor shall meet them daily, and they shall receive, in addition to such other instruction as he may give them, his system of lectures on Polemic Theology, and shall be exercised by him in the writing of theses in divinity, as he shall from time to time assign them: *Provided,* always, that the Professor shall be careful to examine the students in such way as he shall judge most advisable, upon the substance of every lecture delivered by him.

4. It shall be the duty of the Professor to direct the attention of the students to the reading of such works, on the several subjects, as they occur in his lectures, as he may think calculated to give them full and correct information in relation to all the grand doctrines embraced in the system of theology, and he shall, from time to time, satisfy himself that these works are consulted by them.

5. It shall be the duty of the Professor to prepare a full and copious system of questions upon all the subjects of Didactic and Polemic Theology, which the students shall be obliged to answer in writing at their rooms, and at their leisure, and which shall form the basis of their examination before the Board of Superintendents. Vol. VI., p. 18.

SEC. II. *Recommendations to students.*

Resolved, That it be recommended to the students of our Seminary to study the claims of the destitute parts of our own country, as well as of the world at large; to consider the question of personal duty in regard to them; to acquire due conceptions of the amount and forms of labor requisite in given fields; to spend a portion of their vacations in colporteur labors; and while cherishing a sturdy spirit of endurance, that they cultivate those habits of study, and modes of address, which will facilitate their entrance among them. Vol. VII., p. 427.

SEC. III. *Theological Professors guardians of young men aided by the funds of the Church.*

Resolved, That the Theological Professors be requested to consider themselves guardians of all young men beneficiaries of the Church, watch carefully over their conduct and life, and whenever they discover censurable expenditure, remissness in study, lack of mental or religious qualification, they make, as soon as practicable, a report to the Board of Education. Vol. VIII., p. 582.

SEC. IV. *Re-arrangement of Seminary year.*

Resolved, That the term of the Theological Seminary commence on the twentieth day of September, to continue until the third Tuesday of May, with an interval of eight or ten days at the Christmas Holidays.

Resolved, That the annual meeting of the Board of Superintendents be held on the third Tuesday of May. Vol. IX., p. 20.

SEC. V. *Members must be actually connected with the Classes which they represent.*

Resolved, That no person can be entitled to a seat in the Board of Superintendents who is not at the time being a member of the Classis for which he was elected. Vol. IX., p. 214.

SEC. VI. *A yearly detailed report of every student to be made.*

Resolved, That the Board of Superintendents be requested to adopt some plan by which the Professors of the Theological Seminary will make a yearly detailed report to the Board of Superintendents of every student in the Seminary; and that they be authorized to have blank reports prepared and printed for this purpose. Vol. IX., p. 333.

SEC. VII. *Expenses of members of the Board to be paid by their Classes.*

Resolved, That * * * * * * the expenses of the Board of Superintendents be paid by their respective Classes. Vol. IX., p. 342.

SEC. VIII. *Rules with reference to students' preaching.*

Resolved, That no student of Theology in our Seminary be allowed to preach or lecture in any of our churches and congregations, except that the students of the Senior class be allowed to deliver their own discourses, under the direction of one of the Professors of Theology, with the understanding that this direction is to extend to the time when, the place where, and the discourse to be delivered; and except further, that students of the Senior Class be allowed the same privileges in the churches of which they are members, under the direction of their own pastors, the direction to extend as in the case before mentioned.

Resolved, That the Board of Superintendents, at their annual meeting, inquire of each member of the different Classes whether he has conformed to the above resolution, and embody in their report to this Synod the result of their inquiries, with the names of any that have exceeded the rule.

Resolved, That the Professors of Theology be requested to discourage all preaching of students of Theology previous to their licensure.

Resolved, That the above resolutions are not intended to abridge the liberty or interfere with the duties of the students as private members of the Church and followers of the Lord Jesus. Vol. IX., pp. 345, 346.

A. (*a.*) HERTZOG HALL.

SEC. I. *Standing Committee appointed.*

Resolved, That a Standing Committee on the Peter Hertzog Theological Hall be appointed. (See Sec. III., 1 below.)

Resolved, That this Committee shall have the general charge of this property, to keep it in repair, and attend to such business matters as may be necessary for its proper preservation; and that this Committee shall report fully at each stated session of the General Synod.

Resolved, That this Committee are hereby authorized and requested to secure such additional funds as may be needed to accomplish the objects of the Institution.

Resolved, That the expenditures of the Peter Hertzog Theological Hall, by the Committee of this Synod having the same in charge, shall not in any case exceed the amount of funds actually collected. Vol. IX., p. 215.

SEC. II. *Empowered to make rules for the regulation of the Hall. In case of difficulty references is to be had to the Board of Superintendents.* Vol. IX., p. 448.

SEC. III. *Continued with additional regulations.*

Resolved, That the Standing Committee on the Peter Hertzog Theological Hall, appointed in 1857, and then authorized and directed to secure such additional funds as may be needed to accomplish the objects of the Theological Institution, shall be and hereby is continued under the following additional regulations:

1. The Standing Committee on the Peter Hertzog Theological Hall shall consist of six* members, one of whom shall be appointed by the Theological Faculty from their own number each year, and five of whom shall be laymen, to be elected by General Synod, to be divided into three classes, to hold office respectively one, two, and three years.

2. This Committee shall be and hereby is empowered whenever in their judgment it becomes necessary, to appoint a financial agent or agents for the collection of funds for the endowment and support of the Seminary, and the general advocacy of the interests of the Theological Seminary.

3. This Committee shall pay over the funds collected by them to the Board of Direction, except so much as is necessary for repairs upon the buildings and appurtenances from year to year.

4. This Committee shall hold quarterly, or, if necessary, more frequent meetings at New Brunswick, during the term time, on such regular and fixed days as it may select.

5. This Committee shall be the Executive Committee of the Board of Superintendents as now constituted, shall report annually to said Board at its annual meeting for the examination of students, and shall be under the general direction of said Board.

6. This Committee shall hold a joint session together with the Board of Superintendents, at the annual meeting at New Brunswick, for the full consideration of the temporal interests of the Theological school.

7. The Board of Superintendents shall report to the General Synod, at its annual sessions, the result of the

* Number as changed by Synod in 1868. Vol. XI p. 645.

action of the above Committee, under the above regulations. Vol. XI., p. 478.

B. THEOLOGICAL SEMINARY AT HOLLAND.

SEC. I. *Preliminary arrangements.*

At the meeting of General Synod in June, 1866, there was presented

"A memorial from the members of the Senior Class of Hope College, respectfully petitioning the General Synod to take such measures as may enable them to pursue their theological studies at their present institution."

On this application Synod

Resolved, That the subject be referred to the Board of Education and the Council of Hope College, with instruction that leave be granted to pursue their theological studies at Hope College, provided no measures shall be instituted by which additional expense shall be thrown upon Synod or the Board of Educatiou at this time; and provided further, that Synod reserves the right to withdraw this permission at any time that it may deem expedient. Vol. XI., pp. 96, 97.

SEC. II. *Council of Hope College to act as Board of Superintendents.*

Resolved, That the Council of Hope College be and the same is hereby constituted and appointed the Board of Superintendents of the Theological School in Hope College, with duties and prerogatives like those of the Board of Superintendents of the Theological School at New Brunswick. Vol. [illegible], p. [illegible].

C

C. RUTGERS COLLEGE.

SEC. I. *Articles of Agreement between Synod and Trustees modified.* Vol. VII., p. 418.

SEC. II. *Board of Direction empowered to convey title to College property at New Brunswick to Trustees.* Vol. X., p. 471.

SEC. III. *Synod relinquishes the nomination and appointment of Professor of Theology, provided it does not interfere with contract in relation to moneys made up for salary.* Vol. X., p. 628.

SEC. IV. *Synod informed that Board of Trustees accedes to above.* Vol. XI., p. 265.

D. HOPE COLLEGE.

SEC. I. *Holland Academy taken under the care of the Synod.* Vol. VIII., p. 363.

SEC. II. *Title of property confirmed to Synod.*

No. 64. (House)
STATE OF MICHIGAN, 1863.

"The People of the State of Michigan enact that the General Synod of the Reformed Protestant Dutch Church, a body corporate under the laws of the State of New York, is hereby authorized and shall have the capacity to have, receive, hold, and enjoy by gift, grant purchase, devise, or other legal or equitable form of conveyance, the real estate and premises in the County of Ottawa and State of Michigan, known as the Holland Academy, and the grounds connected therewith, for the purposes of said Academy, and their appurtenances; and the sale of said property heretofore made to said

Church is confirmed. And, also, any other real estate that may be conveyed to said corporation for educational purposes.

Provided, that said corporation shall not continue to hold any real estate in this State, not actually occupied by it in the exercise of its franchises, for a longer period than ten years." Vol. X., p. 253.

SEC. III. *Plan of support and supervision.*

TITLE OF THE PROPERTY.

This is now confirmed by an act of the Legislature of Michigan, as invested in the General Synod for educational purposes. Hence arises the obligation of the Synod to provide means to meet all such expenditure as may become needful in the preservation and management of the property.

THE FUTURE SUPPORT OF THE ACADEMY

Must claim the care of General Synod, and until it can be sustained by more permanent endowments, must be supported by such adequate though temporary expedients as Synod may devise.

It is proposed that for the present and until, by endowment or otherwise, the academy may become self-sustaining, that the salary of the Principal, Professors and teachers be provided for through or by the Board of Education.

That, so long as this arrangement or dependence may continue, the Board of Education shall have the appointment of the Principal, Professors and teachers.

PLAN OF SUPERINTENDENCE IN A BOARD OF SUPERINTENDENTS.

In order to a more efficient supervision of the Academy and the increase of its usefulness and influence, the Particular Synod of Chicago shall nominate and the General Synod shall appoint a Board of Superintendents, composed of at least *two ministers* and *one elder* from each of the Classes of the Particular Synod of Chicago. Of this Board, the Secretary of the Board of Education, and the Principal of the Academy, shall be ex-officio members.

THE OFFICERS OF THE BOARD

Shall be a President, Secretary, Treasurer, who shall be annually chosen by ballot.

TERM OF SERVICE.

At the first meeting of the Board the requisite steps shall be taken to divide the members into three classes to serve one, two, and three years respectively.

EXTENT OF CONTROL.

The supervision of this Board shall be to attend the annual examination, and make a report concerning it; to examine the Academy accounts, and have a general care of the interests of the institution; and, so soon as the dependence of the Academy upon the Board of Education shall cease, such supervision shall extend to all matters pertaining to the Academy; such as the appointment of teachers, regulating their salaries, and causing them to be paid, the course of instruction, examinations, repairs, alterations, and improvements of the buildings used for educational purposes, the use and cultivation of the grounds.

REPORT TO SYNOD.

The Board of Superintendents shall annually report

to General Synod their proceedings during the year, and append to the same the account of the Treasurer of the Academy, duly audited, and the names of the members whose term of office is about to expire.

QUORUM.

A quorum, for the transaction of business, shall consist of five members.

SPECIAL MEETINGS

Of the Board of Superintendents may be called by the President, or he shall call the same on the written application of two of its members.

WAYS AND MEANS.

That the Academy may be placed on a permanent basis, the Board of Superintendents are requested immediately to initiate measures for its endowment in the sum of $30,000. The funds which may be raised for the endowment, shall be paid over to the Board of Direction of General Synod, and by it, safely invested for the exclusive benefit of the Institution. The interest accruing from the endowment fund shall be used for the payment of the salaries of the professors or teachers, and for contingent expenses. The tuition fees and incidental expenses shall be fixed by the Board of Superintendents, and the proceeds shall be used by them for the benefit of the Institution. Vol. X., pp. 320–321·

SEC. IV. *Endowment as a College directed.*

Resolved, That, as speedily as possible, Holland Academy should be endowed as a first-class College in the West. Vol. X., p. 466.

SEC. V. *Arrangement for securing a College Charter.*

Resolved, That in order to enable the Board of Superintendents of the Holland Academy to obtain a College Charter, under the law of the State of Michigan, when they shall have obtained subscriptions in good faith to the amount of $30,000, with twenty per cent. thereon paid in to the Board of Direction, they shall receive from the Board of Direction a proper instrument, donating to them the said subscribed amount of thirty thousand dollars. And, that by this act of General Synod, the Board of Direction is instructed and empowered to prepare and deliver such instrument. Provided, however, that the said instrument shall contain such covenants and conditions between the Board of Superintendents of the Holland Academy and the General Synod, that all the rights and interests of the General Synod, as acknowledged in the existing relations between them, shall be and remain undisturbed. Vol. X., p. 484.

SEC. VI. *Vacancies during intervals of Synod.*

Resolved, That the Board of Superintendents of our Western College have power to fill vacancies occurring in its numbers during the intervals of Synod. Vol. X., p. 623.

SEC. VII. *President to make a supplementary report to Synod.*

Resolved, Inasmuch as the Board of Superintendents of our Western College meets after the yearly session of General Synod, and thus its report presents a statement nearly a year old, that the President of said College be requested to supplement the above-named report with such additional information as shall furnish to the General Synod a statement of the condition of said College for the current year. Vol. X., p. 623.

SEC. VIII. *Articles of Incorporation.*

Articles of Association for the Incorporation of Hope College at Holland, in Ottawa County, in the State of Michigan.

We, the undersigned, associate together to become a Corporation for the purpose of founding and establishing a College under the laws of the State of Michigan, entitled "An Act to provide for the Incorporation of Institutions of Learning," approved February 9th, 1855, and of the acts amended thereto.

The name of the Institution is Hope College. The Trustees and their successors are to be a body corporate, and their corporate name is "The Council of Hope College."

The location of the College and the Corporation is at Holland, in Ottawa County, in the State of Michigan.

The character and object of the College and of the Corporation are to provide the usual literary and scientific course of study, in connection with sound evangelical religious instruction, according to the standard of the Reformed Church, as based on the Holy Scriptures. Although the College is denominational in its character, yet students shall be admitted to all its advantages without reference to their ecclesiastical connections, subject only to the general rules and regulations of the Institution.

The Trustees or Council may, at their option, conduct a Theological Department for the training of Missionaries and Ministers of the Gospel, and also a Normal

Department for the training of teachers. The Grammar School, composed of the preparatory classes, shall remain a permanent part of the College, under the supervision of the Council of the College.

The amount of funds on capital stock donated or given to the Trustees or Council for the said College, is as follows:

The General Synod of the Reformed Church in America, a body corporate under the laws of New York, and authorized to hold property for educational purposes in the State of Michigan, has in good faith and in due form donated or given to the said Trustees or Council for the purpose of endowing this College, the sum of thirty thousand dollars, of which sum six thousand dollars has been already paid to the Associates or Trustees for the use of this College. In addition to this the said General Synod has set apart for the use and purposes of this College and Incorporation, the real estate and premises in the County of Ottawa and State of Michigan, known as the Holland Academy. And moreover, the said General Synod, as a body corporate, holds in express trust for this Corporation and College (independent of the aforesaid thirty-thousand dollars, already donated and heretofore set forth), in subscriptions, promissory notes, and cash, twenty thousand dollars, and which sum is from time to time becoming increased by donations.

The following are the names and places of residence of the Trustees, and the length of time of their continuance in office:

Philip Phelps, Jr., Holland, Ottawa County, Michigan, *ex-officio* member as President of the College, while President, but not to exceed 30 years.

John L. See, New Brunswick, New Jersey, *ex officio*

member as Corresponding Secretary of the Board of Education, R. C. A., while such Secretary, but not to exceed 30 years.

John Mason Ferris, Flatbush, Long Island, New York, until September 1st, 1866.

Solomon Cummings, Centreville, Michigan, until September 1st, 1867.

Samuel James Rogers, Geneva, N. Y., until September 1st, 1868.

Schuyler Colfax, South Bend, Indiana, until September 1st, 1869.

John S. Joralmon, Fairview, Ill., until September 1st, 1865.

John N. Rogers, Davenport, Iowa, until September 1st, 1867.

Cyrus G. Van Der Veer, Davenport, Iowa, until September 1st, 1868.

Edward P. Livingston, Bushnell, Ill., until September 1st., 1869.

Seine Bolks, Zeeland, Michigan, until September 1st, 1866.

Hessel O. Yntema, Vriesland, Michigan, until September 1st, 1867.

Peter J. Oggel, Holland, Michigan, until September 1st, 1868.

Arie Cz Kuyper, Pella, Iowa, until September 1st., 1869.

N. D. Williamson, ——————, until September 1st, 1866.

Jacob Van Zanten, Low Prairie, Ill., until September 1st, 1867.

John Van Der Meulen, Milwaukee, Wis., until September 1st, 1868.

Roelof Pieters, Alto, Wisconsin, until September 1st, 1869.

The manner in which the succession of Trustees shall be secured, and the successers of the present Trustees elected, is as follows:

The person appointed as President of the College, while he continues to hold such office as President, shall be *ex-officio* one of the Trustees or Council of the College. The person who holds the situation of Corresponding Secretary of the Board of Education of the Reformed Church, while he continues to hold such office, shall be *ex-officio* one of such Trustees or Council.

The Particular Synod of Chicago (hereinafter described), shall appoint one permanent member of said Board of Trustees or Council, who shall hold his office for thirty years, provided his ecclesiastical relations to said Synod shall so long continue. But if those relations close, his office shall be vacated, and the Synod may appoint a successor to him on the like terms and conditions.

The other members of the Board of Trustees or Council (not exceeding in the aggregate, with the above designated President and Secretary and permanent membeis. the number of thirty-five), shall be chosen by appointment and confirmation of the General Synod of the Reformed Church, on nomination of the Particular Synod of Chicago, the latter being an ecclesiastical body constituted under the Constitution and Laws of the said Reformed Church.

It is composed of representatives of several Classes, being an inferior ecclesiastical organization of said Church.

The Council of Hope College is to be constituted from four members of each of the Classes belonging to said

Particular Synod. So long as the number of said Classes shall not exceed eight, the Council is to be constituted of four members from each of them, the full term of office of each member being four years.

They are to be divided into four parties or sets, so that one fourth of the whole number may go out of office each year. Vacancies occurring in the intervals of the meetings of the Synod, so that they cannot be filled by nomination and appointment as herein provided, may be filled by the Council. And the acting members of the Council shall continue to be Trustees until the appointment shall be made as herein provided.

In case the number of Classes shall be increased, so that the selection of four members from each of them shall in the aggregate exceed the number of thirty-two, then said Particular Synod may apportion the members among the several Classes in their discretion, so as to reach and not exceed the number of thirty-two.

Under the foregoing Articles, we, the undersigned, do hereby associate for the purpose of forming a corporation under the name and for the objects aforesaid.

Philip Phelps, Jr.,	John L. See,
A. C. Van Raalte,	Schuyler Colfax,
P. J. Oggel,	John Mason Ferris,
S. Bolks,	A. C. Kuyper,
Hessel O. Yntema,	J. S. Joralmon,
C. G. Van Der Veer,	N. D. Williamson,
E. P. Livingston,	Solomon Cummings.
R. Pieters,	Samuel. J. Rogers,
J. Van Zanten.	

STATE OF NEW YORK, } *ss.:*
City and County of New York, }

Albertus C. Van Raalte, Philip Phelps, Jr., and John

Mason Ferris, three of the subscribers to the above articles of association, do each for ourselves swear that the amount of stock, thirty thousand dollars, mentioned in the foregoing articles of association, has been in good faith subscribed for such College, and that twenty per cent., namely six thousand dollars, thereof has been paid in, in cash.

A. C. VAN RAALTE,
PHILIP PHELPS, JR.,
JOHN MASON FERRIS.

Sworn to this 26th day of April, 1866, before me,
JULIUS M. POMEROY,
[L.L.] Commissioner of Michigan in New York.

STATE OF MICHIGAN,
Office of the Secretary of State, } *ss.:*

I, George H. Hanse, Deputy Secretary of the State of Michigan, do hereby certify that I have compared the annexed copy of the Articles of Association of the "Hope College" with the original, filed in this office May 14th, 1866, and that it is a correct transcript therefrom, and of the whole of such original.

In testimony whereof, I have hereunto set my hand and affixed the Great Seal of the State of Michigan, at Lansing, this fourteenth day of May, in the year of our Lord one thousand eight hundred and sixty-six.

Great Seal of the State of Michigan. (1835).

GEORGE H HANSE,
Deputy Secretary of State.

{STAMP 5cts.}

SEC. IX. *Changes in arrangement of Council agreed to.* Vol. XI., p. 90.

CHAPTER VIII.

FUNDS OF THE CHURCH.

Treasurer's Digest is annually published in the Minutes of General Synod.

SEC. I. *Means of meeting Deficiency.*

Resolved, That the amount necessary to be raised in order to meet such deficiency as there may be in the revenues of Synod, be hereafter assessed directly by the General Synod upon the Classes, and that the Treasurer transmit to the General Synod an estimate of the amount necessary to be raised, which document shall be placed in the hands of the Committee on the Board of Direction, who shall make the apportionment, and present the same to the Synod for adoption, which Synodical assessment shall be transmitted by the Stated Clerk to the several Classes. Vol. XI., p. 414.

A. WIDOWS' FUND.

SEC. I. *Plan of the Fund as amended.*

1. The Fund shall be called "The Fund for the Relief of Disabled Ministers, and the Widows and Children of Ministers of the Reformed Church," and shall be administered by the Board of Corporation of the General Synod of said Church, during the pleasure and under the control of the General Synod.

2. Every minister of the Reformed Church may secure a full interest in the Fund, by the payment of $20

annually. Payments of ten dollars, or five dollars, annually, shall entitle subscribers to a proportionate benefit from the Fund. Neglect of payment for one year to be a forfeiture of privilege. Interest, however, shall at all times be required after six months. Payments at one time, of a sum, the interest of which, at four per cent. per annum, shall amount to twenty dollars, or to ten dollars, or five dollars per annum, shall give a claim upon the Fund in the same manner as if those amounts were paid annually; and, in this case, the amount of the original payment may, at the death or disability of the minister, be withdrawn, without impairing the right of benefit from the Fund. Ministers interested in the Fund, by the payment of an annual subscription, shall be at liberty to relinquish such interest by ceasing to make such annual payment; and they, as well as those who have heretofore ceased to make such payments, shall be entitled to receive seventy five per cent. of the amount paid by them, without interest, by giving notice to the Treasurer nine months prior to the thirtieth day of April in each year, provided the amounts so to be paid shall not, in the aggregate, exceed one-half of the income of the current year; in which case one-half of such income shall be distributed *pro rata* among the applicants, and the balance due them shall be included among the applications for payments to be made at the close of the next fiscal year. Ministers who have made a payment of a principal sum, as above provided, may withdraw the amount of money actually paid by them, without interest, by giving nine months notice to the Treasurer prior to the thirtieth day of April in any year, and shall be entitled then to receive the same from the principal of the Fund. Ministers leaving our Church shall be subjected to the same rule in the withdrawal of their subscriptions.

3. One-half of the annual payments by Ministers, and donations, when so specially directed by the donor, shall be considered income; the other half of the annual payments by Ministers, all other donations, and the collections in the Churches shall be considered principal, and the interest only used as income. There shall also be added to the principal, at the close of each fiscal year, out of the income, a sum equal to three per cent. of the principal sums standing to the credit of individual Ministers, in consequence of payments made by them under the provisions of paragraph two. Consistories or individuals may, at their pleasure, direct their contributions, collections and donations, to apply in whole or in part to the credit of any minister they may designate; but in such cases the same shall be considered as principal, and not thereafter withdrawn, unless otherwise directed at the time of payment.

4. No money belonging to this Fund shall be loaned (except on temporary loan with collateral security) unless secured by bond and mortgage on real estate. The moneys belonging to this Fund shall be kept separate and distinct from all other funds of Synod.

5. The officers of the Board of Corporation shall be the officers of the trust—the Treasurer's duty shall be to collect the income and make all payments. He shall report minutely and fully to General Synod at each of its annual meetings; his accounts to be audited by a committee of the Board of Corporation.

6. The maximum amount to be paid to parties interested in the Fund shall be—to a minister disabled by sickness or age, two hundred dollars per annum; to the widow of a deceased minister, two hundred dollars per-

annum; to children of clergymen, both whose parents have deceased, seventy-five dollars per annum, each, until they attain the age of sixteen years. Should the income, upon due experiment, be found to admit it, this maximum may hereafter be increased. When but one payment has been made, the maximum of the annuity allowed shall be seventy-five dollars. When two annual payments have been made, the maximum annuity allowed shall be one hundred dollars. When three annual payments have been made, the maximum annuity shall be one hundred and fifty dollars. When four annual payments have been made, the maximum annuity shall be one hundred and seventy-five dollars; and where payments have been made for five years and upwards, the maximum annuity shall be, as above stated, two hundred dollars—the widows and children of such to receive respectively according to this graduation.

As long as the income is sufficient to pay each claimant the maximum annuity, the maximum shall be allowed; but should the income not be sufficient, then the whole income shall be divided among the claimants in proportion to their claims.

It is expressly understood that in all the above cases, to entitle the applicants to their annuities, the payments of subscriptions must be continued regularly until they cease by the operation of the principles herein contained.

7. A widow of a minister contracting marriage, forfeits her claim to the annuity—but in such case the children under sixteen years of age shall be entitled to their annuities, as though both parents had deceased.

8. In disbursing the income of the Fund, where a minister is the applicant, he shall be required to produce a certificate from his Classis, or other satisfactory

evidence, declaring that by reason of sickness, old age, or other providential cause, he is incapable of service.

Where a widow is an applicant, like satisfactory evidence of the decease of her husband, and the date thereof, shall be required.

When children, both whose parents have deceased, are concerned, like evidence of the death of their parents, and of their own age, shall be required.

9. The payments to annuitants shall be made half yearly; to ministers, commencing with the date of their incapacity for service; to widows, from the death of their husbands; and to children, from the death of their last surviving parent.

The Treasurer's books, on authentic vouchers, shall furnish the evidence of the payment of subscriptions.

Annuitants shall be admitted to the benefit of the Fund by a vote of the Trustees of the Fund, or a committee specially appointed for that purpose.

10. Alterations may be made in the rules relating to the general management of the Fund, by a vote of two-thirds of the paying subscribers thereto; but the plan, in its essential principles relating to a civil compact between each subscriber and the General Synod, as the contracting parties, cannot be altered without the consent of every paying subscriber.

11. These rules are adopted and confirmed by Synod, as the system for the management of the Widows' Fund. Vol. X., pp. 497–500.

Sec. II. *Classes to induce Churches to secure an interest for their pastors.*

Resolved, That the different Classes be requested to adopt measures to induce the churches under their care to appropriate the regular annual sum to secure their respective pastors an interest in the fund. Vol. VIII., p. 610.

SEC. III. *Classes to appoint a member to solicit supscriptions or collections.*

Resolved, That each Clasiss be directed to appoint one of its members to solicit subscriptions or collections for the Widows' Fund within the bounds of such Classis, either by personal interviews with Consistories, or by preaching upon the subject; and that the person so appointed be considered an officer of General Synod to act in this behalf. Vol. X., p. 204.

SEC. IV. *Classes to carry out plan of agencies for.*

Resolved, That this Synod enjoin upon all the Classes undcr their care to carry out the plan of Classical agencies in behalf of the Widows' Fund, adopted in 1863, with all practicable promptness and fidelity, and earnestly commend the Fund to the Churches. Vol. X., p. 496.

B. DISABLED MINISTERS' FUND.

SEC. I. *Plan of the Fund.*

1. The Fund shall be called "The Disabled Ministers' Fund of the Reformed Church," and shall be administered by the Board of Corporation of the General Synod of said Church, during the pleasure and under the control of General Synod.

2. The Board of Direction shall keep securely invested such contributions as by the special direction of the donors are to be kept as principal, and the interest only to be used.

3. Should there be at any time more money belonging to the Fund than may be immediately required, the

same shall be deposited on interest in the New York Life Insurance and Trust Company, or in the United States Trust Company, in the city of New York; or it may be loaned on the stocks of the City, or State of New York, or of the United States.

4 The Fund, with the income of that part of it which, in accordance with special donations, is to be kept invested, shall be used for the support of disabled ministers, and the families of deceased ministers, *when such may be in need.*

5. Applications for aid must be accompanied by a satisfactory recommendation from the Classis to which the applicant belongs, certified by the clerk thereof, and stating the amount needed.

6. The Board of Direction are authorized to make grants on such applications, and it shall present a full report of the receipts, disbursements, and proceedings of the Board, with a statement of the Fund, and the treasurer's account duly audited, each year, to the General Synod.

7. The treasurer shall take charge of the money as received, and make all payments.

8. The Classes are requested to take proper steps to give effect to the action of the General Synod on this subject.

9. All of the Churches under the care of the General Synod are requested to take up a collection yearly for the Fund. Vol. X., pp. 271–272.

C. CHURCH BUILDING FUND.

SEC. I. *Plan of the Fund.*

1. All benevolent Funds for Church Building purposes, however raised, shall be paid into the hands of

the Treasurer of General Synod, and shall be held by the Board of Corporation as a Church Building Fund, and shall be dispensed by the Board of Domestic Missions at its discretion.

2. Applications for aid from this Fund shall be made to the Board of Domestic Missions, under recommendation of Classis, and the amount required stated, as also the amount to be raised by the people asking such assistance.

3. A first bond and mortgage shall be executed by the Board of Corporation, to be made payable in one year by any Church receiving an appropriation. The interest thereon may be remitted at the discretion of the Board of Domestic Missions, and in case of such remission, the Church shall make a yearly collection for the Fund; and every Church aided shall be expected to pay back the aid received as soon as practicable.

4. No Church shall be aided which would have a debt remaining after receiving assistance from this Fund.

5. An annual collection shall be solicited from all the Churches towards this Fund. Vol. X., pp. 201–202.

Resolved, That the Building Fund of the Church, and all future contributions thereto, be committed to and received by the Treasurer of the Board of Domestic Missions, and that the future disposition of that fund, and all investments thereof, be made by and under the direction of that Board, subject to the rules and regulations now in force touching its investment and distribution, with this modification, that the amount of advances and the time when they shall be made to Churches in course of erection be in the discretion of the Board, to be executed by them in view of all the circumstances surrounding each case respectively, the Board being careful to take the accustomed and approved security in the case of each advance as heretofore practiced in the administration of the fund. Vol. XI., p. 281.

SEC. II. *Moneys solicited for Churches &c., to be secured to the denomination.*

Resolved, That it be recommended to all Churches which shall solicit pecuniary aid for the erection of church edifices and parsonages and for the purchase of land or other property for Church uses, to take all proper legal measures to secure such property to the possession of the Reformed Church, and especially to provide, in case of the alienation of said churches from our denomination, that the amount so collected from individuals and congregations of the Reformed Church shall be returned to the Board of Direction of the Reformed Church, to be granted by them upon similar terms, with the advice and consent of the Board of Domestic Missions, for the erection of church edifices for needy congregations, under the care of said Missionary Board.

Resolved, That the contributors to such enterprises be recommended to affix the same terms to their gifts. Vol. IX., p. 575.

CHAPTER IX.

CHURCH GOVERNMENT.

SEC. I. *Order of Judicial Business.* (See Rules of Order of General Synod, p. 21.

SEC. II. *Lower judicatories must act under the laws.*

Resolved, That every inferior judicatory is bound to

act under the laws of the Church, until they shall have been regularly and constitutionally changed. Vol. V., p. 504.

SEC. III. *The mode of dissolving a church relation.*

It is an established principle of church government, that the relation subsisting between a church and its members can be dissolved only by death or dismission, or an act of discipline. Withdrawing is, therefore, out of the question. 1824, p. 46.

SEC. IV. *The Synod will not legislate on abstract questions.*

Application for advice having been made by a Classis, in relation to a certain case, the Synod declared itself decidedly of the opinion, that it is wholly inexpedient to legislate upon abstract questions. and adopted this resolution:

Resolved, That this Synod do not consider it proper to express their opinion in the case, and leave the Classis to adopt such measures, in accordance with the discipline of the Church, as in their wisdom they may think proper. 1824, p. 46.

SEC. V. *Ministers and members, on removing; to transfer their relation within one year.*

1. *Resolved,* That it be enjoined on ministers to transfer their Classical relation to the Classis within whose bounds they may at any time remove, within one year after the time of such removal.

2. *Resolved,* That it be enjoined on members of our Churches, to transfer their relation to the Church in our connection or in correspondence with us, within whose bounds they may remove, within one year after their

removal, if such removal place them from under the supervision of the Church of their previous connection Vol. III., p. 363.

SEC. VI. *Deputati Synodi.*

Resolved, That whenever a *deputatus,* regularly notified, finds himself unable to attend, that he be bound to give notice of the same, as soon as practicable, to the President of Classis. Vol. V., p. 59.

Resolved, That it be enjoined on the church at whose call the Classis shall convene to attend an examination, to pay the necessary expenses of the *deputatus,* that this consideration may not operate to embarrass him in the discharge of his duty. Vol. IV., p. 496; Vol. I., 1797, p. 7; 1815, p. 73.

Resolved, That the several Classes be directed to yield a strict compliance to the rule of the Constitution, in relation to the presence of a *deputatus* at examinations. Vol. V., p. 58.

SEC. VII. *The subjects of Baptism.*

1. The right or privilege of infant baptism doth not rest upon what is called full communion, nor is the partaking of the Lord's Supper, by one or both of the parents, an indispensable test for admitting infants to be baptized in the Reformed Church.

2. In avoiding one extreme which straightens admission into the Church of Christ, by making a test not commanded in the word of God, it is necessary to watch against the opposite evil, which makes no distinction between the pure and vile, and which, by an indiscriminate administration to all who apply, relaxes Christian discipline and prostitutes the sacred ordinance of baptism. The General Synod, therefore, recommend

and enjoin that when both the parents openly profess such errors or heresies, or are chargeable with such immoralities and improper conduct as ought, if they were in full communion, to exclude them from the table of the Lord, they shall not, during such apostacy in doctrine or manners, be permitted to present their infants to baptism; but shall be denied that privilege until they profess repentance and show amendment. When one of the parents shall be thus guilty, and the other is a decent and peaceable professor of the religion of Jesus Christ, the infant shall be baptized at the request and upon the right of the professing parent, who alone shall stand and present the child. And lastly, where the minister and one or more of the elders find great ignorance in the parents, and such a want of knowledge in the first principles of our holy religion as to render them unfit to make a public profession of their faith, it shall be their duty to withhold them for a time, notwithstanding their decent moral conduct and profession, and frequently and affectionately instruct them previous to their admission to the ordinance, that thus, if possible, the confession and vows at the baptism of their infants may be made with knowledge, sincerity and truth. 1804, p. 6, (See, also, 1816, p. 25, and Vol. IV., p. 287.)

Sec. VIII. *Ministers without charge.*

Resolved, That the several Classes be advised to the utmost strictness, in requiring ministers not declared *Emeriti*, or disabled by infirmity, or conscientiously engaged in the education of youth, diligently to exercise their sacred functions, and to command those who, without good reason, have engaged in worldly business, if any such there be, that they return to their duty, under penalty of the discipline enjoined by the Church for such offences. Vol. VII., 1846, p. 68.

SEC. IX. *Candidates.*

1. Every candidate upon coming within the bounds of any Classis, shall, after the first Sabbath, call on a Standing Committee of Appointments, which shall be made by said Classis, and receive instructions before he proceed to preach in their vacancies.

2. Each Classis shall enter upon their Minutes a lemma respecting candidates, and every candidate shall be bound (if practicable) to attend the meeting of the Classis under whose jurisdiction he may at any time be found. Vol. I., 1797, p. 11.

SEC. X. *Professor of Theology.*

Whereas it is necessary that the ecclesiastical relation of the Professor of Theology should be clearly ascertained and settled by General Synod, as well for the information and guidance of the Professor, as of the several judicatories of the Church; therefore,

Resolved, That, by the Constitution of the Reformed Church, the Professor of Theology, as such, has no relation to or connection with any particular Classis, and is amenable only to the General Synod, whose officer he is, and of course must take a regular dismission from the church and Classis to which he belonged: but whenever he shall sustain, or with the consent of the General Synod assume, the pastoral charge of a congregation, he will, as pastor, stand on the same footing respecting the Classis with which such congregation is connected, as any other minister of a congregation. Vol. I., 1814.

Sec. XI. *Rights of ministers in collegiate churches.*

In answer to the question "whether in collegiate and chartered churches the ministers have, or have not, a vote and a seat in the consistories of such churches?" Synod advised that, for preserving peace and harmony in the respective churches, each consistory to whom the question applies, inquire into their practice in times past, and adhere strictly to the same in all time to come, without attempting to introduce any alteration or innovation. 1797, p. 13.

Sec. XII. *Baptized children to be transferred with their parents.*

Resolved, That in the transfer of the parents from one section of the Church to another, the membership of their baptized children be recognized, and they be included in such transfer. Vol. IX., p. 191.

Sec. XIII. *Provisions for payment of assessment for contingent expenses.*

Resolved, That every Consistory be advised, at the meeting held for the appointment of a delegate to Classis, to furnish to the minister or delegated elder the sum assessed to pay the Contingent Fund of General Synod.

Resolved, That the Classes be requested to impress upon their Questors the duty of reporting to them such churches as fail to meet their obligations to the Contingent Fund.

Resolved, That Synod recommend that they introduce a standing rule that each pastor be required, at the annual spring session of Classis, to state the reasons for any deficiency in that department, in case such dereliction should exist. Vol. IX, p. 447.

SEC. XIV. *Stated Clerks of Classes to fill the column of " Total in Communion."*

" Your Committee find it to be a general rule that the churches without pastors are represented as having no member," &c.

Resolved, That the Stated Clerks of the several Classes be directed to fill up the blanks in the column headed " Total now in Communion " by inserting the number in the last Report, so signifying the fact. Vol. X., p. 314.

SEC. XV. *Directions for Consistorial Reports.*

For the sake of promoting uniformity.

Resolved, 1. That in the Consistorial Report under the head " *Number of Families,*" only such be reckoned as are attendants upon the services of the Church.

2. That the several Consistories be directed to keep a separate list of those members whose places of residence after diligent search, cannot be ascertained, and that such members be not included in the yearly statistical report.

3. Under the head of " *Catechetical and Bible Classes,*" by Catechumens be understood only such as are regularly instructed in the catechisms recognized by the Church ; by " Biblical Instruction," be understood such only as are instructed directly from the Bible as a text book.

4. Under the head of " Contributions for Religious, Congregational, and Benevolent Purposes," be under stood the actual contributions of the congregations to said objects for the year thus reported, excluding all income from bequests of previous years, rentals from real estaie, or invested funds of whatever kind.

5. That the above rules be printed on the backs of the statistical tables for future guidance. Vol. XI., p. 80.

SEC. XVI. *Ministers and Consistories to have the collections ordered by Synod taken up.*

Resolved, That it is the duty of every settled minister, and of every Consistory where there is no settled pastor, to see to it that the collections ordered by Synod are regularly taken up in the churches under their care. Vol. XI., p. 504.

CHAP. X.

DOCTRINES AND MORALS.

SEC. I. *On the marriage of a deceased wife's sister.*

Whereas, the rule prohibiting the marriage of a man with his deceased wife's sister is found only in resolutions passed by General Synod at its previous sessions, (see Vol. I., 1797, p. 12; 1815, p. 32; 1816, p. 23; Vol. III., p. 59,) and not in the Constitution of the Reformed Church; and whereas a majority of the Classes have reported against such rule, therefore,

Resolved, That all resolutions which may have been passed by the General Synod, forbidding a man to marry his deceased wife's sister, be and hereby are rescinded. Vol. VI., p. 221.

SEC. II. *On dancing.*

Whereas, the mingling in promiscuous assemblies for the purpose of engaging in the amusement of dancing, as usually conducted, is exclusively worldly in its nature and tendency; and, on the part of professors of religion, is calculated to dissipate seriousness, unfit the mind for devotion, and lower the dignity and spirituality of the Christian character and profession; is adverse to the growth of grace and the abiding influence of the Holy Spirit in the churches; is calculated to conform the Church to the world, grieve and offend its members, and place a stumbling-block in the way of the conversion of sinners; while such practice is generally regarded in the light of a dividing line between the Church and the world; therefore,

Resolved, That this Synod regard it as inconsistent with the nature and design of the Christian profession, and ought neither to be indulged in by professors of religion nor countenanced in others.

Resolved, That it be enjoined on pastors and consistories, with all kindness and fidelity, and by all suitable means, to discountenance the practice of this and all similar amusements at variance with the dignity and sobriety of Christian deportment. Vol. VI., p. 344

SEC. III. *Catechetical instruction.*

Whereas, it appears from the statistical tables of the different Classes that catechetical instruction is greatly neglected in certain sections of the Church, therefore,

Resolved, That the different Classes be directed to give their special attention to this subject, so that, as far as possible, the youth in all our congregations may enjoy the benefit of pastoral catechetical instruction, according to the provisions of the standards of our Church. Vol. V., pp. 59–60.

SEC. IV. *Intemperance.*

The following resolutions were unanimously adopted by the General Synod in 1828: *Resolved*—

1. That the principle adopted by many individuals and societies in different parts of the country for the suppression of intemperance, viz: total abstinence from the use of ardent spirits, excepting only its use as a medicine, meets with the decided approbation of this Synod.

2. That it is therefore earnestly recommeneed to the members of our churches that they entirely refrain from the use of ardent spirits, except as above mentioned.

3. That it be requested of all our ministers and churches to inculcate the said principle, not only by example but by precept, and especially among the rising generation, and to diffuse such information as may be deemed best calculated to effect the object.

4. That it be recommended to our churches, ministers, and individual Christians, to promote the cause of temperance by the formation of societies, or by such other measures as may be thought best adapted to the end.

5. That, as without God we can do nothing, the prayers of all Christians be requested for his blessing upon the means used, and for the putting forth of his power for the suppression of intemperance. Vol. III., p. 133.

SEC. V. *Sabbath observance.*

Resolved, That this Synod regard with deep interest the extensive and awful profanation of the Sabbath in this country.

Resolved, That this Synod consider the running of public stages, and steamboats, and canal boats on the Sabbath, a gross profanation of that holy day, and that the members of our churches and congregations be and hereby are earnestly solicited to discourage, both by counsel and example, all such travelling on the Sabbath day.

Resolved, That it be and hereby is recommended to our different Classes and congregations to take the subject of the Sabbath into their serious consideration, and to devise such measures as may, under the divine blessing, prevent the profanation and promote the sanctification of the Sabbath-day. Vol. III., pp. 73, 114, 262; Vol. VI., p. 192.

SEC. VI. *Disapproval of "Mercersberg Theology."*

Resolved, That this Synod do hereby express, in the most decided and unequivocal manner, their protest against all those sentiments of a Romanizing character and tendency which are technically known as the "Mercersberg Theology," as being essential departures from the faith, as calculated to lead yet farther astray from the old landmarks of truth, and to undermine the great principles of the Reformation from Popery. Vol. VIII., p. 319.

SEC. VII. *Ministers to prevent betting and games of chance as unscriptural.*

Resolved, That it is enjoined on all ministers, in their public ministry, to set forth the unscriptural character of betting and all games of chance, and the evils which naturally flow from them, and that Consistories be enjoined to act in their official position to discountenance and prevent the use of lotteries in disposing of goods at church fairs. Vol. XI, p. 86.

CHAPTER XI.

CUSTOMS AND USAGES.

SEC. 1. *Essential and non-essential customs.*

Synod adopted the following report:

Agreeably to the resolutions of the Particular Synod of New York, in May last, Art. 11th, under the lemma, *Customs and Usages;* and also Art. 27th, under the lemma, *Instructions to Delegates:* The first resolution requiring "that the President inquire of the delegates of the different Classes present, whether such customs and usages as are tested by long experience to be for edification, and whether the injunction of watching against innovations, are attended to in the respective churches under their care." The second resolution requiring "that our delegates to General Synod be directed to inquire of that body, to what particular objects the inquiries respecting customs and usages are to be directed by the different Classes." Your committee beg leave to report, that those customs and usages which were deemed necessary to be continued in the Church, are expressed in the explanatory articles of the Constitution; such as singing the psalms and hymns approved of, and recommended by General Synod; preaching from the Heidelberg Catechism; observing the forms in the administration of baptism and the Lord's Supper, &c., as contained in our Liturgy, &c. That other customs and usages prevail in the Church which are deemed non-essential, and in many instances are either wholly dispensed with or partially retained in our congregations, according to the taste or circumstances of pastors or people; such as the arrangements observed in the performance of public worship; the number of times singing psalms and hymns; reading sermons, and preaching them from memory or extemporaneously; sprinkling in baptism, one or three times; sitting or standing in receiving the Lord's Supper; preaching on Ascension Day, Good Friday, and other days which have long been observed both in Holland and America, &c. Your committee observe that those customs and usages which are deemed essential and constitutional, are preserved pure and entire by the different Classes; and we observe likewise, that those which are considered non-essential are dispensed with or retained and altered, according to the taste or circumstances of different ministers and congregations. 1814, pp. 31, 32.

SEC. II. *Of the forms of the Church.*

The following report was adopted:

The committee to whom was referred the subject of the use of the forms by our churches, beg leave to report; that in the third chapter of the Constitution, article first, under the head of Customs and Usages, they find this subject is legislated upon as far as at present necessary or expedient. Uniformity in our modes and forms of worship, so far as the same is obviously contemplated by the Constitution, your committee believe to be important, and ought to be required of all our churches; and they recommend that the several Classes be enjoined to adopt prompt measures to secure the observance of these forms in all the churches under their care. Vol. V,, p. 389.

Resolved, That the Stated Clerks of the several Classes be requested to send, annually, a copy of their statistical report to the Stated Clerk of General Synod. Vol. III., p. 183.

SEC. III. *Revision of the Sacramental Forms of Liturgy not adopted.*

Resolved, That inasmuch as the revision of the Sacramental Forms has several times been sent down to the Classes for their action, and a large majority have either failed to report, or have reported against any alteration, in the judgment of this Synod the Church has decided to make no revision.

The last General Synod passed a resolution authorizing the Board of Publication to have printed those forms in the Revised Liturgy which the Synod have not acted upon, and to allow ministers and Consistories to use them or not as they may choose. Four Classes have endorsed this action, and recommended the adoption of these forms ; four have approved in part, but the great majority have either passed by the subject in silence, or have disapprovéd of the addition. Vol. IX., pp. 330, 331.

SEC. IV. *In coöperation with others, our standards to be guarded.*

Resolved, That this Synod does not depart from its uniform practice of making no declaration of abstract principles. It leaves the subject of union with other denominations, in their efforts to promote revivals of religion and the edification of the Church, to the prudence of ministers and Consistories, with the advice that they take care that the attachment of the people to our doctrinal standards and our usages be not impaired. Vol. IX., p. 507.

SEC. V. *Catechetical instruction and preaching.*

Whereas, In order to preserve the truth and promote the prosperity of the Church, it is of the highest importance that the children should be trained in the knowledge and love of sound doctrine, and that the catechism should regularly be *explained* in our churches ; therefore,

Resolved, That the General Synod earnestly calls upon the Consistories under its care to see that the catechetical instruction of the children is faithfully attended to, not only by pastors and teachers, but also that parents be continually reminded of the obligations resting upon them to instruct and bring up their children in the doctrines taught in our Church to the utmost of their power, in accordance with the covenant which they solemnly made with God and His Church, when they presented their children for baptism.

Resolved, That the attention of Consistories, Classes, and Particular Synods be directed to Article II., Section 13, of the Constitution, which requires every minister, within certain periods of time, regularly to explain the system of Christiån doctrine comprehended in the Heidelberg Catechism, and which also directs censure to be inflicted in case any minister should fail to comply therewith, without sufficient reason. Vol. X., p. 618.

CHAPER XII.

CORRESPONDENCE WITH OTHER CHURCHES.

SEC. 1. *The subject in general.*

It is the ardent desire of this Church to maintain friendly and fraternal relations with all evangelical churches, and especially to be in close and perfect union with those who adopt and maintain our own formularies, or others of kindred spirit and form. Vol. VI., p. 186.

SEC. II. *Correspondence with the Presbyterian Church.*

BRIEF HISTORY OF.

A correspondence between the two Churches was organized in the year 1785, contemplating a meeting of representatives from the respective Churches for the purpose of fraternal consultation. In the year 1797 a committee was appointed by the General Synod to confer with committees from the General Assembly of the Presbyterian Church and from the Associate Reformed Synod, to form some more definite plan of mutual correspondence and intercourse. In the year 1800 a plan of correspondence was submitted to Synod from these committees, embracing the communion of particular churches, the friendly interchange of ministerial services, and a correspondence of the several judicatories of the conferring Churches. As some of the details of this plan did not accord with the views of Synod, they declined fully to accede to it. A friendly correspondence, however, appears to have been maintained between the Churches until the year 1822, when the following plan was adopted:

1. Any member of either Church may be received in communion to the other, on producing to the proper church officers sufficient evidence of a good and regular standing in the church with which he is connected. Vol. II., 1822, p. 47.

2. It shall be permitted to the competent church officers in any congregation, settled or vacant, to invite to

their pulpit any minister or probationer who is in good standing in either of said Churches, and who preaches in their purity the great doctrines of the gospel as they are stated in their respective Confessions of Faith, and have generally been received and taught in the Reformed Churches; but it shall be entirely optional to give or withhold such invitations; nor shall it be esteemed offensive or unkind if the invitation be withheld. *Ibid.*

3. A vacant congregation shall be at liberty to call a minister from either of the Churches, according to the order established in the Church from which he may be called, he conforming himself to the order of that Church; and in case of a congregation being formed of people from both, it shall be at liberty to put itself under the care of either, at its option. *Ibid.*

4. Persons under censure or process of censure in either Church shall not be received into the other Church while such censure remains, or such process is unfinished. *Ibid.*

5. The ministers of one of the corresponding Churches shall not in any case intrude upon the office of the ministers of the other Church.

6. None of the inferior judicatories shall be at liberty to admit to their respective bodies or under their care any student or licentiate from the sister Church, without a regular dismission from the ecclesiastical body or theological seminary to which he is considered as attached. Vol. III., p. 255.

7. The General Assembly of the Presbyterian Church and the General Synod of the Reformed Church shall each appoint one minister, with an alternate, as a delegate to these judicatories. 1822, p. 48; Vol. VI., p. 73.

Sec. III. *Privileges of Delegates.*

Resolved, That this Synod consider the articles of correspondence adopted between the highest judicatories of the two Churches as authorizing the delegates from each of these judicatories mutually to deliberate on all questions that may come before them, in the same manner and to the same extent as their own members, subject to the rules of both houses; and that the said delegates are excluded only from the privilege of voting. Vol. II., 1822, p. 32.

Sec. IV. *Correspondence with the R. D. Church of S. Africa, and the Waldenses in Piedmont.*

Resolved, That Synod open a correspondence by letter, and accompanied by our Annual Minutes, with the Synod of the Reformed Dutch Church in South Africa, and the Synod of the Waldenses in Piedmont. Vol. VIII., p. 536.

Sec. V. *With the Free Church of Scotland.*

Resolved, That this Synod are gratified to receive the intimation that the opening of a correspondence will be acceptable to the Free Church of Scotland, and cordially accede to such an arrangement. Vol. IX., p. 15.

Sec. VI. *With the German Reformed Church.*

Resolved, That in pursuance of the recommendations of the above report, this Synod appoint delegates to * (both the General Assemblies of the Presbyterian Church) and to the Synod of the German Reformed Church. Vol. X., p. 277.

* Both reunited this year, 1869.

SEC. VII. *With the Reformed and the United Presbyterian Churches.*

Your Committee recommend that such correspond ence be opened. Adopted by Synod. Vol. X., p. 424.

SEC. VIII. *With the Canada Presbyterian Church.*

The Committee recommend that this request (the appointment of a delegate) and that General Synod reciprocate the fraternal salutations of the Canada Presbyterian Church. Vol. XI., p. 583.

CHAPTER XIII.

RELIGIOUS NEWSPAPERS.

SEC. I. *Board of Publication to issue a Monthly.*

Resolved, That this Synod approve the proposition made by the Board of Publication, to issue a monthly paper for ecclesiastical purposes. Vol. VIII., p. 614.

SEC. II. *The Boards of the Church to use it and bear a just proportion of the expense.*

Resolved, That the several Boards of our Church be recommended to employ the columns of * "*The Sower*" in communicating to the Churches knowledge of their respective operations, and that it be further recommended that each Board bear so great a proportion of the expenses of that paper as may seem to it to be just. Vol. IX., p. 118.

*The monthly referred to in Sec. 1.

SEC. III. *Pastors and Consistories to endeavor to secure its introduction into every family.*

Resolved, That each Pastor and Consistory of our denomination are requested by General Synod to make an especial effort to secure the introduction of " *The Sower*" into every family of their respective Churches. Vol. X. p. 645.

SEC. IV. *A Weekly paper essential.*

Resolved, That the General Synod consider a weekly newspaper to be essential to the interests of the Church. Vol. VIII., p. 285.

SEC. V. *An incorporated company to be formed for publishing one.*

Resolved, That it is desirable to have among us a religious newspaper of such a character and so ably conducted that it shall find entrance into every family of our Church, and secure also a fair outside support.

Resolved, That in order to secure further this intended circulation, all the members of our church should have an opportunity of becoming interested in its support, instead of its being conducted for the profit of any individual or company.

Resolved, That we recommend the formation of an incorporated company under the general laws of New York, with a capital stock of not less than twenty thousand dollars, ($20,000,) of which any member of any of our congregations shall have liberty to take $100 and over, which corporation shall establish and conduct such Paper.

Resolved, That General Synod recommend such a Paper to the support of the Church, on condition that the certificate of corporation of such company shall provide that all the profits realized therefrom exceeding ten per cent. per annum upon the capital stock shall be paid over at the expiration of each year as follows, viz.: One-half thereof to the Disabled Ministers' Fund, the interest of which, and so much of the principal as may be required, shall be annually appropriated under the established regulations of the Fund, and one-half thereof to the Board of Domestic Missions, to be added to the Church Building Fund, and on this further condition, that every certificate of any share or shares issued for stock in said company shall contain a provision that no sale or transfer thereof shall be made until an offer of sale of the same at par value shall be made to the Board of Direction.

Resolved, That a Special Committee of five Elders, consisting of James Myers, John Lyon, James A. Williamson, Lewis Applegate, and S. R. W. Heath, be appointed to carry out these views of Synod as speedily as possible.

CHAPTER XIV.

PARTICULARIA.

Sec. I. *Union of Church and State.*

Resolved, That that part of the 36th article of the Confession of Faith, as now printed, which declares that it belongs to the office of the civil magistrate "to protect the holy Church service, and to prevent and extirpate all idolatry and false worship; to destroy the kingdom of Antichrist; to promote the kingdom of Jesus Christ, and to take care that the word of the Gospel be preached everywhere, that God may be honored and worshiped by every one as He commands in His Word," is sufficiently explained in the preface of the Constitution and 35th explanatory article.

Resolved, That the Reformed Church deprecates any union between Church and State as alike detrimental to the interests of vital piety, and dangerous to that liberty of conscience which is now enjoyed by the citizens of our happy Republic.

Resolved, That the results of experience in this country abundantly prove that the Church needs no other support than the piety of its members and the grace of Christ. Vol. IV., pp. 438–439.

SEC. II. *Funeral Service.*

A form for this service having been introduced to the attention of Synod, "after mature deliberation the motion passed in the negative, as far it respects the limitation to any prescribed form; but the Synod approve of speaking a word in season, either at the grave or in the house, or the church, and to close the solemnity with a prayer and benediction. 1812, p. 34.

SEC. III. *Days of special Humiliation and Prayer.*

Resolved, That whenever, in any of our churches, religion is in a low and declining state, it is recommended as a very important duty, and under the divine blessing made the means for the revival of religion, to observe the season usually set apart preparatory to the administration of the Lord's Supper for the purposes of special humiliation and prayer. 1826, p. 36.

SEC. IV. *Psalm-book not to be a source of profit.*

Resolved, That this Synod regards the general diffu sion of our book of Psalms and Hymns, as an ob ject much more desirable than any pecuniary profits that may be derived from the publication or sale of the book, to whatever object these profits may be devoted.

Resolved, That the Board of Corporation be requested to effect the reduction of the price of our Psalm-book as soon as practicable. Vol. IV., p. 439. See also Vol. VII., p. 96.

SEC. V. *Sacred Music.*

Resolved, That it be recommended to our several Classes to pursue such measures as they in their wisdom shall judge best for exciting attention to sacred music, in order to elevate its standard in their respective churches.

Resolved, also, That the introduction of music in our district schools be recommended. Vol. V., p. 421. See also Vol. IV., p. 533, and Vol. V., pp. 89–92.

SEC. VI. *The Act of the New York Legislature in regard to religious incorporations.*

Resolved, 1. That this General Synod consider the Act of the Legislature as opposed to the practice, injurious to the interests, and subversive of the Constitution and rules of government of the Reformed Church.

2. That all our churches be, and they are hereby enjoined against adopting the provisions of said Act, and that the churches which have already adopted them be directed to dispense with them and adhere to the Constitution and orders of the Church.

3. That the Elders, P. D. Vroom, Stephen Van Rensselaer, John D. Keese and Abraham Van Nest, and the Rev. Andrew Yates, D. D., be appointed a committee to confer with the church at whose request it was passed, and those churches which may have adopted its pro-

visions, as to the expediency of requesting its repeal. Vol. IV., 1835, p. 437–438.

This committee reported the next year (1836) that they had met with a committee of the consistory of the church referred to, and had had a full and free conference with them in relation to the Act and the expediency of procuring its repeal, but had not been able to come to any specific agreement or understanding:

Whereupon, it was *Resolved,* That this General Synod do still entertain the opinion expressed at their last meeting, as to the effect of the law upon the Constitution of our Church and its permanent welfare. And they do most earnestly and affectionately advise and recommend to the congregations and consistories that have availed themselves of its provisions, to adopt such measures in relation to it as will best tend to remove existing embarrassments, promote the harmony and order of our Zion, and preserve the purity of its principles and faith. Vol. IV., p. 533.

SEC. VII. *Report on the State of Religion to be read from the pulpit.*

Resolved, That it be recommended to the different ministers to read from their pulpits the Report of the Committee on the State of Religion; and also such parts of the Report of the Committee on the Professorate as they shall consider important to be known by all the churches, upon the first Sabbath after the printed Minutes shall be received, or as soon thereafter as practicable. Vol. III., p. 210.

SEC. VIII. *Titles to be omitted in recording names in Minutes.*

Resolved, That all distinctive titles or appendages to the names of members of Synod be omitted in recording the Minutes of this Synod; such distinctive title being prefixed or appended to the name of the member in the 'list of members constituting the Synod. Vol. VII. p. 507.

SEC. IX. *Column for Contributions in the Statistical Tables.*

Resolved, That the present column for contributions embrace only those that are strictly benevolent; and that a column for congregational purposes be added, which shall include all moneys raised for salaries, debts, church expenses, etc., and that, if necessary, the column headed "Total of the Congregation" be dropped. Vol. IX., p. 56.

SEC. X. *Stated Clerk to distribute Minutes to Institutions.*

Resolved, That the Stated Clerk of Synod have twenty-five copies of the Minutes of Synod at his disposal, to be distributed among literary and theological institutions. Vol. IX., p. 244.

SEC. XI. *Expenses of Delegates from Western Classes.*

Resolved, That we return to the arrangement of 1857, viz: to divide the sum appropriated between not more than three delegates from each Classis; and if there be less than three delegates in attendance, then each delegate shall receive but one-third of the sum thus appropriated. Vol. IX., p. 467.

SEC. XII. *Minutes of Synod to be published and circulated as soon as practicable.* Vol. XI., p. 83.

Sec. XIII. *Article* XIII *of Minutes altered to "Church Colleges."* Vol. XI., p. 91.

SEC. XIV. *"Theological School" in Constitution changed to "Schools."* Vol. XI., p. 340.

SEC. XV. *"Hymns of the Church" approved and recommended.*

Resolved, That General Synod approve and authorize the book entitled "Hymns of the Church," including the ninety-five additional hymns, for which approval is asked, and recommend it to all churches, families and individuals within their communion.

Resolved, That the action of General Synod in 1848, prohibiting the issue of any edition of the Psalms and Hymns of our church without the Confession of Faith and Liturgy, be re affirmed in relation to the "Hymns of the Church" approved by this Synod.

Resolved, That the Committee having this matter in charge be instructed to procure a sufficient number of copies of said book for use in our Churches, which shall contain our Doctrinal Standards and Liturgy, as now published, and that General Synod recommend such only to be introduced into our Churches.

Resolved, That all such copies shall bear upon their title page the name of our Church "Reformed Church in America." Vol. XI,, p. 641.

SEC. XVI. *Reports of Delegates to corresponding churches not to be printed in Minutes.* Vol. XI., p. 419.

SEC. XVII. *New Hymns approved and publication authorized.* Vol. XI., p. 468.

SEC. XVIII. *Classis of Holland permitted to translate and publish the Constitution in the Hollandish language.* Vol. XI., p. 497.

APPENDIX.

PARTICULAR SYNODS.

In view of the entirely remodeling effect of the action of General Synod at the meeting in 1869, since it is not all actual law until part of it has received the sanction of the Classes, and the Synod so enact it, yet is so soon in all probability to become law, it is deemed best for the present edition simply to place the resolutions adopted by Synod in an appendix. Parties interested in the matter will be in no danger of mistake. Whatever is not affected by this new action still abides. Whatever is so affected is of course modified or superseded by this later action. A mere pencil mark in each one's copy, after the action of the Classes is made known, will secure all needed correctness. The action of Synod is as follows :

1. *Resolved*, That this Synod deems it desirable to organize a new Particular Synod, and that the Classes of Bergen, South Bergen, Monmouth, New Brunswick, Paramus, Passaic, Philadelphia, and Raritan, be and hereby are dismissed from the Particular Synod of New York, to constitute a new Particular Synod.

2. *Resolved*, That the Classes of Bergen, South Bergen, Monmouth, New Brunswick, Paramus, Passaic, Philadelphia, and Raritan be and hereby are instructed to appoint delegates at their next fall sessions, in conformity with the provisions of the Constitution, to meet in the First Reformed Church of New Brunswick, N. J., on the first Monday of November next, at 10 o'clock, A. M., and proceed to organize a new Particular Synod, to be called the Particular Synod of New Brunswick.

3. *Resolved,* That the Revs. Goyn Talmage, J. Elmendorf, and Gabriel Ludlow, be a Committee on the part of this Synod, to attend the above-mentioned meeting, and assist in the organization of the contemplated Particular Synod.

4. *Resolved,* That the Classes of Kingston and Orange be and hereby are transferred from the Particular Synod of Albany, to the Particular Synod of New York.

5. *Resolved,* (If a majority of the Classes concur), That every Particular Synod shall hereafter consist of a delegation of four Ministers and four Elders from each of the Classes within its bounds.

6. *Resolved,* That it be enjoined upon the Particular Synods to transact their business with due deliberation, and to hold such devotional services during their sessions as may conduce to the spiritual improvement of their members, and the several Churches in which they assemble; and that to compass this desirable result, it is earnestly recommended by this Synod, that the Particular Synods hereafter convene at three o'clock, P. M., of the day designated for their regular session; that after their organization is effected, the first hour be spent in devotional services; that the Synodical sermon be preached the same evening; that the first hour of the next morning session be spent in devotional exercises, in connection with which the Chairman of the Committee on the State of Religion shall read such extracts from the annual reports of the Classes as he may elect; that in the afternoon of the second day of the session, the Lord's Supper be administered under the auspices of the Synod; that in the evening of the same day a sermon be preached before Synod; the Preacher and his theme, together with an alternate, to be chosen at the preceding annual session, and that the first half hour of each

subsequent day of the Synod be spent in devotional services.

7. *Resolved*, (If a majority of the Classes concur), That the Particular Synods be, hereafter, Courts of final appeal for all causes that have, in accordance with the provisions of the Constitution, been tried originally in the Consistory, unless as many members of the Particlar Synod as there are Classes composing said Synod shall, within ten days after the adjournment of the same, file with the President of the Particular Synod a certificate to the effect that in their judgment, any cause originating in the Consistory which has been reviewed by the Particular Synod, is a proper case for the action of the General Synod, in which case an appeal may be taken to the higher judicatory.

8. *Resolved*, That two committees be hereafter appointed by each of the Particular Synods, to be called respectively the Committee on Church Visitation, and the Committee on Church Extension; that each of these Committees be composed of nine members, viz: Six Ministers and three Elders; that at the next regular session of each of the Particular Synods, these Committees be appointed by ballot—one-third of their number, viz: Two Ministers and one Elder being chosen to serve for one, two, and three years respectively, and that at each succeeding annual session, two Ministers and one Elder be elected for three years.

9. *Resolved*, That the Committee on Church Visitation be charged with the promotion of spiritual religion and Christian beneficence among the Churches within the bounds of the Particular Synod; and that at some suitable period of each year, it arrange to hold a Convention of Churches within the limits of each Classis, at which some of its members shall be present, to urge

these important interests upon the minds and hearts of the people.

10. *Resolved,* That the Committee on Church Extension be charged with the general supervision of our denominational growth within the bounds of the Particular Synod; that it search out opportunities for the establishment of new organizations, and that it afford all possible encouragement and assistance to feeble enterprises—it being understood that this Committee is designed to supplement rather than supersede the efforts of the Classis, and the Board of Domestic Missions, and that nothing in this resolution shall be construed in such a manner as to infringe the prerogatives of either.

11. *Resolved,* That the Secretaries of the several Boards of the Church be requested, so far as they may be able, to attend, alternately, the sessions of the Particular Synods, and address the members upon the claims of the respective Boards, and upon the general subject of Christian beneficence.

The plan, thus suggested by your Committee, involves the necessity of amending two sections of the Constitution. They recommend, therefore, the adoption of the following supplemental resolutions, viz:

Resolved, That the General Synod approve and propose to the Classes the amendment of Chapter II., Article IV., Section I., of the Constitution of the Reformed Church, in such a manner as that it shall read as follows, viz: "Every Particular Synod shall comprehend a certain number of Classes to be designated by the General Synod, and shall consist of a delegation of four Ministers and four Elders from every Classis within its bounds, and nine Ministers and nine Elders, when regularly convened, shall constitute a quorum for the transaction of business, excepting those Synods which may consist of not more than five Classes, in which cases six Ministers and six Elders may form a quorum."

Resolved, That the General Synod approve and propose to the Classes the amendment of Chapter II., Article I., Section 7, of the Constitution of the Reformed Church, by inserting after the phrase "enjoys the same privilege" the language "except that the Particular Synod shall be a Court of final appeal for all causes that have, in accordance with the provisions of the Constitution, been tried originally in the Consistory," unless as many members of the Particular Synod as there are Classes composing said Synod shall, within ten days after the adjournment of the same, file with the President of the Particular Synod a certificate to the effect that in their judgment any cause originating in the Consistory which has been reviewed by the Particular Synod, is a proper case for the action of the General Synod, in which case an appeal may be taken to the higher judicatory.

BY-LAWS OF THE BOARD OF DIRECTION.

The By-Laws of this Board as printed on pages 35 and 36, were transferred from the Digest of 1848. That they were superseded by a new enactment as early as 1827, escaped notice until it was too late to correct the error in the body of the work. The only remedy was to insert them in the Appendix.

The General Synod in pursuance of the authority vested in them by their act of Incorporation, have made and ordained the following By-Laws, to regulate the conduct of the President, Directors, and Treasurer of the Corporation.

I.

The Board shall hold stated meetings at least once in every month, and the President may call special meetings whenever he deems it necessary, and shall call such meetings when thereto requested by any two of the Directors.

II.

A majority of the Board shall constitute a quorum to transact business, and in the absence of the President the attending Directors may appoint a President *pro. tem.* to preside at their meetings.

III.

The Board of Directors are empowered to direct the collection of all moneys which may be due to the General Synod or subject to their control and outstanding, whenever the Board shall consider it necessary or expedient; and also to require new or additional security for outstanding debts, as a condition of extending the time of payment of any such debts which may not be deemed perfectly secure; and all securities for moneys belonging to or under the control of Synod shall be made payable to the Corporation in its corporate name and its assigns, either on demand, or at a day certain, not beyond a year from their date, with interest payable yearly.

IV.

The Board of Directors shall appoint two of their number, who with the Treasurer shall form a Finance Committee, whose duty it shall be to invest or loan the moneys whichs may come into the Treasury over and above the sums required to satisfy any existing claims or appropriations made, as they shall deem safe and most productive, and the Treasurer shall, whenever the amount received into the Treasury exceeds $500 over said existing claims and appropriations, immediately report such excess to the Finance Committee.

V.

The money as they become due shall be receivable by the Treasurer, whose duty it shall be to deposit the same forthwith in the Bank of New York, or in such other Bank as the Board of Directors shall from time to time determine, and all such deposits shall be entered in a book to the credit of the Treasurer of "The General Synod of the Reformed Protestant Dutch Church," who shall have the custody of said book, and all moneys shall be drawn out of the Bank by written or printed checks signed by the Treasurer in his official capacity.

The Treasurer shall keep regular books of accounts, in which he shall enter all moneys received or paid out by him under appropriate heads, designating the particular fund to which the same belong, when and from whom received, and when and to whom paid; and also to keep in said books a particular statement of all moneys loaned, to whom, when, and upon what securities loaned, and all moneys otherwise invested, and when and how; and shall state separately under the head of Donations, all sums of money which have been or may be placed at the disposal of Synod, designating the donors' names, the amount of their several donations, and the particular purposes for which made; and shall exhibit his books of account, including his bank-book, to the Board of Directors for their inspection at every stated meeting, and oftener if requested. And it is made the duty of the Board to examine such books when so exhibited, and to make a brief entry of the general result of the examination in their minutes.

VI.

The Board of Directors are authorized to appoint a Secretary, whose duty shall be to attend their stated meetings and keep regular minutes of their proceedings, and to correspond with such persons as the Board shall direct relative to their business.

VII.

The Board shall report to Synod at their annual meetings, a particular statement of the situation of the funds belonging to or under the control of Synod, how secured or invested, together with such suggestions and information as the Board may deem necessary, the better to secure the said funds, or to render the same more productive; and shall accompany such report with a general abstract of the Treasurer's accounts of receipts, and payments for the past year.

VIII.

The Board is authorized to affix the common seal of the Corporation, and cause their President to give his official signature to any letter of attorney for the collection of debts, or any other purpose, in order to the due fulfilment of any of their aforesaid duties.

IX.

The appointments of the President, Directors and Treasurer shall not endure longer than one year, or until others are appointed, but no new appointments may be made within the year, and the Board of Directors are authorized to suspend the Treasurer from office for misconduct; in which case, or in case of his resignation, death or inability to perform the duties of his office, and also in case of his declining to accept his office, (when thereunto appointed by General Synod, and after their adjournment) the Board of Directors may appoint a Treasurer *pro. tem.* to hold his office until the next meeting of General Synod, and until another Treasurer is appointed.

X.

The Board of Directors are authorized to determine the amount of salary to be paid to the Treasurer and Secretary for their services, (if it shall be deemed by them expedient to grant any salary,) but under this express limitation, that the salary of the Treasurer shall not exceed the sum of $250 per annum, nor shall the salary of the Secretary exceed the sum of $100 per annum, exclusive of necessary disbursements made by them in the execution of their respective duties, to be audited by the Board of Directors; which said salaries shall be paid quarterly yearly if required. And the Board of Direction shall also, from time to time, determine the amount of security to be given by the Treasurer (if any is deemed necessary) for the faithful performance of the duties of his office. And shall also be the judges to determine the sufficiency of the securities offered by him; which bond when executed, is to be left in the custody of the President for safe-keeping.

N. B. This section modified by Synod. See on " Salary of Treasurer," page 30.

XI.

All By-Laws formerly enacted are hereby repealed. Vol. III., pp. 32, 35.

NOTE.—This edition of the Digest is intended primarily as a manual of the legislation of General Synod remaining in force to the present time (1869). The Committee has left out such legislation as has been repealed, or superseded, or has expired by limitation of the subjects concerning which laws were passed. To extend its usefulness, there have been embodied, under their appropriate headings, such permanent historical documents pertaining to the Church as have come into existence since the publication of the last Digest in 1848. Those documents of this character which were embodied in the former Digest, such as histories of the formation of Synods, Boards, &c., are not repeated here, except in one or two instances, on subjects of especial interest. Any who need to consult these will find them in the Digest published in the Minutes of Synod for 1848.

INDEX.

CHAPTER I.

CHAPTER II.

CHAPTER III.

CHAPTER IV.

CHAPTER V.

SYNODS.

A. GENERAL SYNOD.

B. PARTICULAR SYNODS.

CHAPTER VI.

BOARDS OF THE CHURCH.

A. BOARD OF DIRECTION.

B. BOARD OF DOMESTIC MISSIONS.

C. BOARD OF FOREIGN MISSIONS.

D. BOARD OF EDUCATION.

E. BOARD OF PUBLICATION.

F. VARIOUS MATTERS CONCERNING THE BOARDS.

CHAPTER VII.

EDUCATIONAL INSTITUTIONS.

A. THEOLOGICAL SEMINARY AT NEW BRUNSWICK.

A. (*a*). HERTZOG HALL.

C. CHURCH BUILDING FUND.

CHAPTER IX.

CHURCH GOVERNMENT.

CHAPTER X.

DOCTRINES AND MORALS.

CHAPTER XI.

CUSTOMS AND USAGES.

CHAPTER XII.

CORRESPONDENCE WITH OTHER CHURCHES.

CHAPTER XIII.

RELIGIOUS NEWSPAPERS.

CHAPTER XIV.

PARTICULARIA.

APPENDIX.

www.ingramcontent.com/pod-product-compliance
Lightning Source LLC
LaVergne TN
LVHW011213110826
845150LV00006B/1416

* 9 7 8 1 4 2 5 5 1 7 5 5 7 *